Christian Fatherhood

The Eight Commitments of St. Joseph's Covenant Keepers

Christian Fatherhood

The Eight Commitments of St. Joseph's Covenant Keepers

Stephen Wood

with

James Burnham

Family Life Center Publications

Family Life Center Publications
P.O. Box 6060
Port Charlotte, FL 33949

ISBN: 0-9658582-0-0
Library of Congress Catalog Card Number: 97-61528
Book production and design: Tabby House
Cover design: Pearl & Associates
Manufactured in the United States of America

Acknowledgments

We would like to thank our wives, Karen Wood and Lisa Burnham, for their invaluable advice and constant encouragement. We also thank Karen for her suggestion that we work together on this project and for her tireless proofreading. We express special gratitude to Peggy Burnham, Jim's mother, for her extensive editing. We thank Lucy Allen and Hugh Williamson for their help in tracking down resources. Finally, we express our appreciation to Jim and Linda Salisbury of Tabby House for their expertise in helping the Family Life Center publish this book.

Family Life Center Publications
P.O. Box 6060
Port Charlotte, FL 33949

Dedication

To the honor of my father, John Kirk Wood,
and to my sons, John Stephen and Matthew Joseph

A letter of encouragement and support from Mother Teresa

MISSIONARIES OF CHARITY

54A A.J.C. Bose Road
Calcutta 700016 INDIA

"As long as you did it to one of these My least brethren. You did it to Me"

Dear Mr. Stephen Wood and all the St. Joseph's
Covenant Keepers,

God love you for the wonderful work you are doing to
build up families. Families are precious to God; He
loves each family very tenderly. Families are a special
instrument in the hand of God, for it is in the family
first of all that God wants to tell us that we have
been created for greater things -- to love and to be
loved.

Jesus said, "As the Father has loved Me, so I have
loved you. Love one another as I have loved you." So
Jesus is telling us to love each other with the love
of the Heavenly Father. That is why it is so beautiful
that you are building up the family and the Church by
helping fathers of families to love their wives and
children as the Heavenly Father loves Jesus and loves
them. For Jesus, nothing was more important than His
relationship with His Father. And so for every child,
knowing the love of his human father is so important
for learning how to love. Nobody can teach this to
fathers of today better than St. Joseph. He is the best
patron, model and intercessor for the fathers of families.

Be sure to teach the families to pray all together -
father, mother and children. For the family that prays
together stays together, and if they stay together they
will love one another as Jesus loves each one of them.

I am sure that the book "Christian Fatherhood: The
Eight Commitments of St. Joseph's Covenant Keepers"
will be a great blessing to all who read it and put its
teachings into practice. I will be praying that the
Lord will bring peace into the world through the love
of fathers for their families, for works of love are
always works of peace.

Let us pray.

GOD BLESS YOU,

M. Teresa mc.

Contents

Foreword

What has happened to fatherhood? Historically, a father's duties included leading, providing, protecting, and educating. Today, men are abandoning their families in unprecedented numbers.

Four out of ten American children will go to bed tonight in a home without their fathers.[1] By the year 2000, half of all children in America will be raised without their dads.[2]

The two main causes of fatherlessness in our time are divorce and out-of-wedlock births. More than 50 percent of all first marriages will end in divorce; more than 30 percent of babies are born out-of-wedlock.[3] Why? Our world has forgotten God's timeless plan for marriage.

What do Christians mean by marriage? They mean a permanent, heterosexual, sacramental, covenantal union of man and woman, ordered toward the procreation and education of children and the good of the spouses, within which God plays an active role as the third partner.

Every one of these qualities is either controverted or incomprehensible to modern secular culture. In today's world, change is worshipped and permanence is a negative value. Homosexual relationships vie for an equal validity before the law. Sacraments have been pushed aside by aggressive technology and pragmatic materialism. The revocable contract has superseded the irrevocable covenant causing an explosive growth in fatherless families. Children are viewed as products and often liabilities. And the very idea of sanctity in marriage is seen as a parochial religious delusion.

And what of the word "God"? Christians believe in a loving, personal, approachable God whom Jesus Christ addressed as "Abba," that is, "my father." In Christ Jesus and by the power of the Holy Spirit, the God and Father of our Lord Jesus Christ knows each of us by name and wills our eternal happiness. The world rejects this; at best, God is perceived as little more than an impersonal force or universal consciousness without direct involvement in the life of humanity, let alone its individual components.

Finally, without God, there can be no plan, no deeper harmony, to creation. For Christians, all created things have meaning; they are part of a grand symphony giving glory to the Lord of life. But once God, the head and heart of creation, is excised, the symphony becomes discordant. The harmony unravels. The fragments fall apart.

The consequences are enormous. Consider the frightening results of fatherlessness in the United States:[4]

- Sixty percent of rapists, 72 percent of adolescent murderers, and 70 percent of long-term prison inmates come from homes where the father wasn't present.[5]

- The best predictor of violent crime in a neighborhood is the proportion of households without fathers.[6]

- Daughters in single-parent homes are 164 percent more likely to have a baby out of wedlock than girls who grow up in two-parent families, 111 percent more likely to have children as teenagers, and 92 percent more likely to dissolve their own marriages.[7]

- About 90 percent of single-parent homes are without a father.[8]

- Homes with single mothers make up the largest proportion of the population on welfare rolls in the country today.[9]

The world has condemned itself with its own statistics. But the world has no idea where to find lasting remedies for these ills.

Psychology will never develop a therapy to substitute for a loving and faithful father. Prisons cannot replace fathers any more than expensive social programs can. The solution is to restore the vocation of fatherhood so that children will have true fathers.

Fathers are the key to stopping our domestic disintegration. When they decide to heed the teachings of Christ, fathers will solve the crisis in marriage and family life. The fullness of Christianity offers men all the tools they need to lead their families out of the culture of death into the culture of life. And the world will follow the way of the family.

Men—fathers and husbands—are called to respect "woman" in all her specificity. As I wrote in my 1993 pastoral letter to the Church of Denver entitled *Praying with Peter*, in preparation for World Youth Day that same August, "It is essential as we move toward the new millennium that you, my young brothers in Christ, recognize the special urgency of your vocation as men: to be deeply aware, to gaze upon more intensely, to contemplate with greater tenderness the dignity and vocation of woman, of the feminine in all the fullness and complexity of her person" (#38). St. Peter himself teaches in his first letter that husbands are to live with their wives in understanding, showing them honor. In this way, he concludes, the prayers of men arise to God unhindered (1 Peter 3:7). God hears the prayers of men when they are offered with the purity of respect for women.

Pope John Paul II has emphasized the indispensable role of fathers: "Above all where social and cultural conditions so easily encourage a father to be less concerned with his family ... efforts must be made to restore socially the conviction that the place and task of the father in and for the family is of unique and irreplaceable importance."[10] The lay apostolate of St. Joseph's Covenant Keepers is an urgently-needed response to the Holy Father's call to restore Christian fatherhood.

Christian Fatherhood: The Eight Commitments of St. Joseph's Covenant Keepers identifies and addresses the unique needs of fathers. It gives men the practical truths to become faithful husbands and conscientious fathers. This book might have been ignored ten years ago. But the growing awareness of today's crisis in fatherhood and family life is causing people to look beyond superficial remedies. They will find real solutions in this book.

In my forty years as a priest, I have seen again and again that the human heart was made for truth and for beauty and goodness. I have seen that people are hungry for them and will choose them when they are presented clearly and with conviction.

Young people are often dismissed as unresponsive and uncaring when it comes to truth. This myth was exploded by the 1993 World

Youth Day in Denver. The Holy Father ignites millions of young hearts by challenging them with the splendor of the truth. When they hear the authentic proclamation of Christ, undiluted and undiminished, young people respond in faith with an insatiable appetite for God, who is truth. The Holy Father shows us that the high and holy challenge of the Gospel is irresistible.

Fathers are often dismissed as being even more unresponsive than young people. As with youth, we should never underestimate the ability of fathers to respond to Christ. When men hear the noble calling of Christian fatherhood, they will, with the help of God's grace, rise irresistibly to the challenge. *Christian Fatherhood* presents a genuine Christian prescription for renewing the world by restoring the vocation of fatherhood. I pray that every man will read it, and respond courageously.

Archbishop J. Francis Stafford, president
Pontifical Council for the Laity
Feast of the Sacred Heart
June 6, 1997
Rome

"Behold, I will send Elijah the prophet before the great and terrible day of the Lord comes. And he will turn the hearts of fathers to their children and the hearts of children to their fathers...."

(Malachi 4:5-6)[1]

The Heart of Fatherhood

[The heart of fatherhood consists] "in revealing and in reliving on earth the very fatherhood of God."

—John Paul II[2]

It was the best lunch I ever had.

I had been fishing since dawn with my dad and older brother, Kirk, in the pristine waters of one of northern Quebec's most inaccessible lakes. We had gotten up before sunrise, boarded our little fishing skiff, and crossed a ten-mile lake to a shallow waterway concealed in the evergreens. Only a few Native American guides knew of this secret passage, barely wider than our boat. As the sun peeked over the pines, we navigated our craft up the winding channel and emerged at the edge of another large, hidden lake.

At noon we pulled our boat on the deserted pebble beach. There wasn't another person, building, or sign of civilization for miles. For an adventurous ten-year old, to be this far out in the untouched Canadian timberland was almost too good to be true.

We gathered wood to cook our fresh northern pike. Our guide cleaned the fish and pan-fried potatoes in a pound of butter while we sat on logs around a crackling fire. After a full morning of fishing, we all had man-sized appetites. We hovered over the sizzling fillets, our mouths watering. After what seemed like forever, Dad, Kirk and I finally sat down with our guide for an unforgettable feast.

This lunch was the highlight of a week-long fishing trip in a wilderness wonderland. It was unforgettable because I shared it with my dad, away from everything else in the world.

Dad had promised Kirk and me that he would take us on a Canadian fishing trip when we could each swim a hundred yards. Every summer, as little guys, Kirk and I energetically worked on getting up to our required distance. A couple of years after I could finally swim my hundred yards, Dad kept his promise. Kirk and I nearly burst with pride as we crossed the Canadian border for the first time.

One of the surprises of our fishing week in this remote part of Canada was discovering that a group of men from our Pennsylvania hometown shared the other half of our duplex cabin. We were in the middle of nowhere and had virtual neighbors right next to us. These guys had quite a time. They didn't do nearly as much fishing as we did, but boy did they have fun! They had so much fun while away from their wives and families that they were literally falling-down-drunk during their all-night parties. They had so much fun drinking that by the next morning they probably couldn't remember how much fun they had had. But every day about noon they started to remind themselves again. The men from my hometown came home with big hangovers and a modest catch.

In contrast, we came home not only with a station wagon loaded with frozen fish, but with hearts filled with memories that have grown stronger with each passing year. It's been forty years since that lakeside lunch with my father. I've never had a better lunch and never expect to.

The impact of our Canadian fishing trip will last longer than my lifetime. Because of the memories my dad created with me, I also strive to create lifetime memories for my children. It wouldn't surprise me to see my children doing the same with my grandchildren. Fathers should never underestimate the impact they make by spending time with their children. Dad probably never thought that one week spent with Kirk and me in the 1950s would continue to affect future generations. I think that he was just wise enough to realize that making an effort to be with his children pays untold dividends.

What Makes Fatherhood So Important?

Why would a simple fishing trip with Dad leave such an enduring memory? Why would one week with his father forever change a son's life? It seems to defy rational explanation. How do we account for the tremendous influence dads have in the lives of their children? Everyone, even those whose fathers had serious shortcomings, yearns for a perfect father. What makes fatherhood so important?

Fathers leave an indelible impression on their children because their role is linked to another fatherhood. Although this other fatherhood is unseen, every human heart has a deep, insatiable desire to be joined with it. God the Father has made each of us to have a family bond with himself. As a result, the human heart is constantly restless until it is united to the fatherhood of God.

Fatherhood is inescapably religious. Pope John Paul II pinpointed the heart of our role as fathers when he said that our calling is "to reveal and to relive on earth the very fatherhood of God."[3] The Bible says that earthly fatherhood even derives its name from the fatherhood of God (Ephesians 3:14-15). Because they reflect the divine Father, earthly fathers will always influence their children to a degree far beyond reasonable expectations. As fathers we can either greatly speed or impede our children's relationships with the heavenly Father.

Discovering Fatherhood in the Divine Covenant

We discover the heart of our fatherhood in an intimate and personal relationship with God the Father. The Bible calls this family relationship with the heavenly Father a *covenant*. A divine covenant brings a person into a "flesh and blood" family relationship with the Holy Trinity.

The depth of God's love for us in this divine covenant exceeds human comprehension. "See what love the Father has given us, that we should be called children of God; and so we are" (1 John 3:1).

Relax. You don't have to be a religious fanatic to be a good dad. It is often a superficial piety that seeks a super-duper level of spirituality. Theologians tell us that grace doesn't abolish nature; instead, grace works *through* nature. Nothing is more fundamental in nature than marriage and family life. Therefore, we can and should expect the gracious actions of the Holy Spirit to work in and through family life. In supporting, encouraging, and correcting our children, we naturally reflect the fatherhood of God. God works in supernatural ways through ordinary activities with our children like catching fish, playing ball, and landscaping the yard.

To mirror the Father's love, we must first encounter the love of the heavenly Father. As we are shaped by the Father's love, we can eternally shape the lives of our children through the everyday events of family life.

Becoming a Son of God Through Baptism

Our divine sonship begins with Baptism. Unfortunately today, many people underestimate and misunderstand this sacrament. Because original sin (see Genesis 3) spread to the entire human family, we are all born in a state of spiritual death. We need a spiritual rebirth to make us God's children. Jesus said to the Pharisee, Nicodemus, "Truly, truly, I say to you, unless one is born anew [again], he cannot see the kingdom of God" (John 3:3). Nicodemus rightly objected to the possibility of a second physical birth. Jesus then clarified that he meant a *spiritual* birth: "Truly, truly, I say to you, unless one is born of water and the Spirit, he cannot enter the kingdom of God" (John 3:5).

From the earliest centuries, the Church understood this birth by water and the Spirit as referring to the life-giving effect of the sacrament of Baptism. Using slightly different words, St. Paul wrote the same thing in Titus 3:5: "he saved us, not because of deeds done by us in righteousness, but in virtue of his own mercy, by the washing of regeneration [that is, being born again] and renewal in the Holy Spirit."

Prodigal Sons Returning to Their Father

What if we have strayed from the Christian life since our baptism? God has a special sacrament for prodigal sons called the sacrament of Reconciliation. This sacrament is the divine provision for restoring repentant prodigal sons to a relationship with the Father. Since sin is a willful turning away from the Father, we are *all* like the prodigal son. We have turned away from our heavenly Father to pursue pleasures, pastimes, and profits (Luke 15). The first step in returning to a Father-son union with God is repentance. In repenting, we radically turn away from the profound selfishness at the core of our being. We are born self-centered. Our innate selfishness finds expression in an endless variety of sins. Repentance replaces self-will with God's will.

Faith accompanies repentance. "Faith is a personal adherence of the whole man to God who reveals himself. It involves an assent of the intellect and will to the self-revelation God has made through his deeds and words."[4] With faith we place our trust for salvation in God. The Father so loved the world that he sent his Son, Jesus Christ, to take the punishment for our sins by dying upon the Cross. Our personal response of faith in the Father's precious gift of his Son restores us to the family of God. The ruler of the universe becomes our loving Father because of Christ's death for us on the Cross.

In this the love of God was made manifest among us, that God sent his only Son into the world, so that we might live through him. In this is love, not that we loved God but that he loved us and sent his Son to be the expiation for our sins (1 John 4:9-10).

Joining the Father in the Covenant Meal

If the story stopped here it would be a wonderful ending, but there is a crowning gift in our restored relationship with the Father. God doesn't stop with making us members of his family. The Father's love exceeds our every expectation: he extends to us the awesome privilege of sharing in his own divine life.

When the prodigal son returned home, he would have been content if his father had simply let him be a servant within the household. Yet not only did the prodigal son regain the dignity of sonship, but his father provided a special meal to celebrate his restoration (Luke 15:21-24). Meals in biblical times were not like going to a drive-thru at a fast-food restaurant. Meals were special times for creating and renewing covenant bonds among friends and family members. The father's feast was the pinnacle of the prodigal's restored sonship. Sharing his father's meal meant the prodigal fully shared again in his father's covenant life. At this table the formerly estranged son and father became one.

The Most Extraordinary Meal on Earth

The special meal to which the heavenly Father invites all his children is the sacrament of the Blessed Eucharist. Many incorrectly assume that the Eucharist is just an ordinary meal with a spiritual twist. Some think it is merely a symbolic meal; others attach greater significance to it by asserting a spiritual presence of God with the partakers of this meal. However, the Eucharist is much more than this. It is the most extraordinary meal on earth: a Covenant Sacrifice-Banquet. In the Eucharist we share an intimate union with God. The Eucharist literally unites us to God and allows us to share fully in His divine life.

It is of the Blessed Eucharist that Jesus said, "This is my body" and "This is my blood."

> *Now as they were eating, Jesus took bread, and blessed, and broke it, and gave it to the disciples and said, "Take, eat; this is my body." And he took a cup, and when he had given thanks he gave it to them, saying, "Drink of it, all of you; for this is my blood of the covenant, which is poured out for many for the forgiveness of sins"* (Matthew 26:26-28).

Receiving the Fullness of the Father's Life

Jesus instituted the Eucharist at the Last Supper. During this same meal Jesus spoke of the covenant union between God and his children. When Jesus talks about the Father living within his children, we should remember that the context is Eucharistic.

> *"I will not leave you desolate; I will come to you. Yet a little while, and the world will see me no more, but you will see me; because I live, you will live also. In that day you will know that I am in my Father, and you in me, and I in you. He who has my commandments and keeps them, he it is who loves me; and he who loves me will be loved by my Father, and I will love him and manifest myself to him.... If a man loves me, he will keep my word, and my Father will love him, and we will come to him and make our home with him"* (John 14:18-21, 23).

If we obediently keep Jesus' words, then we will experience a oneness with the Father beyond our wildest hopes and dreams. Our union with God is more than an abstract metaphor. God calls us to be joined with him in a "flesh and blood" family bond. It is by receiving the actual flesh and blood of Jesus in the Eucharist that we fully share in the covenant family of God. If we refuse to eat his flesh and drink his blood, or if we minimize the clear teachings of Jesus to fit our rational explanations of the Lord's Supper, then we are cutting ourselves off from full covenant life with the Father.

> *So Jesus said to them, "Truly, truly, I say to you, unless you eat the flesh of the Son of man and drink his blood, you have no life in you"* (John 6:53).

Opening the Floodgates of the Father's Love

Some men who have attended Catholic Masses all their lives may have received little noticeable benefit from the Eucharist. How do we get more from the Eucharist? First, we must get rid of sin which blocks God's grace from coming into our lives. If we are aware of serious sin, we must go to the sacrament of Reconciliation before we partake of the Eucharist. Otherwise, we simply add judgment upon ourselves instead of blessings (see 1 Corinthians 11:27-30). Second, we must come to the Eucharist with an expectant faith. God the Father loves us so much that even if we receive the Eucharist with faith as tiny as a mustard seed, he will flood our hearts with grace beyond all expectation.

"Our Hearts Are Restless Until They Rest in Thee" —St. Augustine

Lunch with my father on the shore of that Canadian lake was a foretaste of an even better banquet. It was an awakening of a deep hunger for a lasting meal with the eternal Father. Sin often warps and twists our desires. What our hearts really seek is a full covenant union with our heavenly Father. The heart cannot stop searching for happiness until it shares life with God in the Blessed Eucharist.

It is from this covenant relationship with the heavenly Father, restored by the sacrifice of Jesus, that we discover the heart of our own fatherhood. Out of the abundance of our divine sonship we discover the strength to become the type of fathers God intends for us to be: earthly fathers reflecting to our children the image of "our Father who art in heaven."

[Jesus] answered, "Have you not read that he who made them from the beginning made them male and female, and said, 'For this reason a man shall leave his father and mother and be joined to his wife, and the two shall become one'? So they are no longer two but one. What therefore God has joined together, let no man put asunder."

—Matthew 19:4-6

An Evangelical Discovers Covenant Keeping

> "To bear witness to the inestimable value of the indissolubility and fidelity of marriage is one of the most precious and most urgent tasks of Christian couples in our time."
> —John Paul II[1]

I had five minutes to decide whether or not to follow Christ.

I had just delivered a sermon on the indissolubility (lifelong permanence) of marriage from the Old Testament book of Hosea. As I sat down during the offertory to prepare my thoughts for celebrating the Lord's Supper, I suddenly realized that I had just preached myself out of the Protestant pastorate. Twenty years of study, preparation, and effort had been undone by a thirty-minute sermon on the covenant of marriage. I had just told my congregation that valid marriages are indissoluble. How could I administer the Lord's Supper to those who had been divorced and unlawfully remarried?

Although my palms began to sweat, my heart was filled with conviction. I realized that as pastor I *couldn't* continue administering the Lord's Supper to those who were in unlawful marriages. Giving communion to people unfaithful to their marriage covenants would be profaning the divine covenant. Receiving the sacrament of oneness between God and his people while being unfaithful to the oneness of the marriage covenant is a sacrilegious contradiction. By

25

giving the Lord's Supper to people in illicit marriages, I would be participating in that sacrilege.

The Holy Spirit was prompting me in the strongest possible manner to stop administering the Lord's Supper immediately. I thought, "Well, I can take some time over the next few weeks to consider this." Yet I feared that God was passing by in a special way, and he was saying, "Come now or never."

The implications of obeying raced through my mind. "I have a wife and five children to support. If I do this I will not only be unemployed, but *unemployable* as a Protestant minister. This is my job, my career, my calling. I have invested over two decades of my life to do this. How can I walk away from my ministry? I must talk to my wife, Karen, first." But God didn't let up. His call was very direct: "Do it *now*."

My stomach knotted; my heart pounded. My shirt felt like a sauna. I stood up and walked to the communion table. I apologized to my congregation and said that I was unprepared to administer the Lord's Supper. They reacted with shocked silence and confused looks. Everyone was wondering why their pastor was "unprepared" to serve them communion. I pronounced a benediction and walked out of the sanctuary.

Voting for Heartache

As a pastor, I had frequently seen the pain and devastation that divorce caused spouses and their children. Regretfully, some of this pain was my fault. Many times in my ministry I had unknowingly lowered Christ's standards for marriage. When I first entered the pastorate fifteen years earlier, the elders of my congregation were split on the question of permitting remarriage after divorce. I'm sorry to say that I cast the tie-breaking vote in favor of allowing remarriage in certain situations. Within ten years, divorce and remarriage had spread through that congregation like wildfire. I saw firsthand that one exception to Christ's norm on the indissolubility of marriage grows into a thousand exceptions until the norm is obliterated.

After study and reflection, I discovered that Scripture, along with the early Church Fathers, taught the indissolubility of a valid marriage.[2]

Our Marriage Covenant and
Our Covenant with God

During the week before my life-changing sermon on marriage, I had been anxiously studying the Old Testament books of Hosea and Malachi. In both books, the Lord speaks forcefully against covenant breaking.

With his unfaithful wife and broken marriage, Hosea was a prophetic picture of Israel's apostasy. The clearest picture God could give to his apostate people depicting their true spiritual condition was the image of an adulterous marriage. Christian teaching about marriage is not the side issue so many people imagine. From Genesis to the close of Revelation, God uses marriage as a picture of his covenant relation to his people. That's why many of the prophets described the apostasy of Israel as "adultery."

While preparing my sermon for that pivotal Sunday, all of my growing convictions about the indissolubility of marriage came to the front of my mind. Previously, I had simply repressed these beliefs. Acting upon them would have enormous implications for my life and for those to whom I was ministering. Many in my congregation were unlawfully divorced and remarried. Even worse, some had done so with my approval and blessing.

Malachi's Ominous Warning

For several months a particular divine warning to religious leaders recorded in the prophet Malachi had been pricking my conscience. Now Malachi's warning was thundering in my heart, forcing me to move beyond my hesitations.

The second chapter of Malachi describes how the Old Testament priests had compromised their sacred duty of proclaiming the truth (2:6-7). By their faulty instruction, these priests had broken the covenant (2:8-9). God lashes these religious leaders with some of the Bible's most ominous words: he will take the *dung* from their sacrifices and spread it on their faces (2:3).

*"Behold, I will rebuke your offspring, and **spread dung upon your faces**, the dung of your offerings, and I will put you out of my presence.... For the lips of a priest should guard knowledge, and men should seek instruction from his mouth, for he is the*

messenger of the LORD *of hosts. But you have turned aside from the way; you have caused many to stumble by your instruction; you have corrupted the covenant..."* (Malachi 2:3, 7-8).

Covenant breaking with God is a spiritual form of adultery. The divine covenant and the marriage covenant are profoundly interconnected. That is why covenant breaking with God often results in covenant breaking with one's spouse and vice-versa.

In Malachi, covenant breaking with God was accompanied by mixed marriages with pagan women and by men breaking covenant with their wives. Middle-aged men abandoning their wives for younger women is not just a contemporary phenomenon.

"...the LORD *was witness to the covenant between you and the wife of your youth, to whom you have been faithless, though she is your companion and your wife by covenant"* (Malachi 2:14).

Notice in Malachi 2:14 that God was the personal witness to the wedding vows. Exchanging wedding vows is not just making a promise or a contract. Rather, it is making a sacred covenant oath in the presence of God. Marriage vows join a man and a woman in a permanent and mysterious oneness paralleled only by our union with Christ.

Responding to Malachi's Rebuke

I realized with shock that Malachi's solemn rebuke to religious leaders applied across the centuries directly to me. Malachi's words triggered a 9.0 "heartquake" on my spiritual Richter scale. I saw that I was giving my pastoral approval to covenant breaking. While most of my Protestant contemporaries felt this was fine, I knew in the core of my being that God was furious enough to smear excrement on my face. Jesus said that a valid marriage was indissoluble. By saying that a lawful marriage could be dissolved in certain circumstances, I was calling evil good.

You have wearied the LORD *with your words. Yet you say, "How have we wearied him?" By saying, "Every one who does evil is good in the sight of the* LORD, *and he delights in them"* (Malachi 2:17).

God's explicit denunciation of divorce in Malachi and Hosea brought me to the end of my shaky rationalizations for covenant breaking. I couldn't continue to minister in a denominational setting that allowed validly married spouses to get divorced and remarried.

Where Do We Go From Here?

After I walked out of the sanctuary, the elders of the church followed me. It didn't take long to explain my actions to them. They agreed that my ministry in that church was over. But I knew it was much more; for all practical purposes, I was leaving the Protestant pastorate forever. Gone were my salary, career, and family's health insurance. What hurt me even more than the financial losses was the disheartening prospect that I had permanently lost the opportunity to preach God's Word.

I remember fighting back the tears as I said to Karen, "Who would ever want me now? Nobody is going to want to hear my beliefs about marriage." When I explained what had happened, I was deeply grateful for the wonderful wife God had given me. Fully aware that we had a very bumpy road in front of us, Karen instantly gave me her unconditional support. Unlike the lone pilgrim in *Pilgrim's Progress*, I had the privilege of traveling toward the Celestial City in the company of my wife.

Now our pressing question was: "Which Christian denomination has preserved the fullness of Christ's teaching on marriage?" There was only one option to consider: the Catholic Church.

Could the Catholic Church Be the Answer?

I never dreamed of becoming a Catholic. On the contrary, I had deep prejudices against what I had perceived to be the Catholic faith. However, my pastoral and theological crisis over the indissolubility of marriage was God's way of shoving me towards Catholicism.

A few days after my sermon on marriage I said to myself, "I wonder what the Catholic Church has to say about marriage." I read for the first time *The Role of the Christian Family in the Modern World* by Pope John Paul II. I was astounded. He expressed such tender care for divorced persons who have remarried, and yet insisted that they refrain from Eucharistic Communion while their state of life contradicts the covenant union between Christ and the Church.[3]

Reading this document, I was struck by its wisdom, its fidelity to Christ's teaching, and its pastoral graciousness. Finally, I had found *the* solid foundation for the survival of the modern family. I was instantly hooked on the Catholic vision of family life. It was so good that I wondered what else the Catholic Church had to say. I was now open for an honest investigation of Catholic teaching.

Surprisingly few Protestant ministers have taken the time to read a handful of books on Catholicism written by Catholics. Like most Evangelical ministers, I had read several Protestant works on why Catholicism was wrong. Yet it was amazing to discover how a dozen books written by Catholics could clarify a mountain of misconceptions about the Catholic Church.[4] Not only do Catholic beliefs have a clear scriptural basis, but they also have an incredibly strong witness in the earliest writings of the Church Fathers.

On July 1, 1990, seven months after I had resigned my pastorate, Bishop John Nevins received our entire family into the Catholic Church at Epiphany Cathedral in Venice, Florida. After receiving the sacraments of Confirmation and the Eucharist, Karen and I also requested the opportunity to renew our marriage vows.

My Road Leads to Rome

Thirty days before entering the Church, I received an unexpected offer. A local businessman volunteered to pay my expenses to go to Rome with Randall Terry, a nationally known pro-life leader, and meet with the Pope.

His offer seemed too good to be true. However, in November 1991, Randy and I attended the first International Pro-Life Summit sponsored by the Pontifical Council for the Family at the Vatican. The pro-life leaders received a special audience with Pope John Paul II.

The Holy Father reminded us that "the family is the sanctuary of life." He warned that our world has embraced a "culture of death" that "is causing a number of deaths without precedent in human history." This culture of death, he said, must be changed. "The first

essential structure capable of doing this is definitely the family."
The family must become the center of our pro-life activity. He stressed
that we must bring the world back to God through the family.

Afterward, each of us was able to greet the pope personally. I
approached the Holy Father with great joy in my heart, and asked
him to bless some rosaries for my family. He did so and also gave me
and my family his apostolic blessing. That meeting profoundly influ-
enced me.

Your Mission, Should You Choose to Accept It...

I came home and pondered the Holy Father's words for a year. I
decided to dedicate my life to his strategy of bringing the world back
to God through the family. I sensed an obvious call to strengthen the
fragile modern family with the practical application of the truths of
the Catholic faith. After collecting 504 dollars in a shoe box at a
family conference, I launched a new apostolate called the Family
Life Center International in November 1992. The purpose of our lay
initiative is to support families worldwide with the historic Christian Faith. The heart of our mission is to cooperate in building a
civilization of love that protects all innocent human life by restoring
the sanctity of the marriage covenant.

For the next two years I piled up frequent-flyer miles speaking
at marriage and family conferences. My audiences consisted prima-
rily of wives wishing their husbands were there, too. It was obvious
that Catholic husbands were not only absent from family conferences, but they were frequently "missing in action" from family life
as well. I saw that the real crisis in marriage and family life today
centers on fathers who have neglected their duties. I sensed a critical need to turn the hearts of Christian fathers to their wives and
children.

Renewing the World Through Fathers

John Paul II has said that the family is the key to "the future of the
world and of the Church."[5] Fathers are the key to the future of the
family. Therefore, it is not an exaggeration to say that the destiny of
the modern world hinges upon the restoration of Christian fatherhood.

The greatest gift any father can give to his children is lifelong fidelity to his marriage covenant. Without the indissolubility of the sacrament of Marriage, fathers will simply not be at home with their children. This is why genuine restoration of fatherhood in our day must include a primary emphasis on marital covenant keeping. Nothing is of more crucial importance for the future of the family.

St. Joseph, God's Chosen Father

At the end of 1994, the International Year of the Family, on the Feast of the Holy Family, I founded St. Joseph's Covenant Keepers (SJCK) to encourage and to equip fathers for service within their families. We chose St. Joseph, the world's greatest father, to be the model for restoring Christian fatherhood.

We want to give men the tools they need to be godly husbands and fathers. We offer them the example of St. Joseph as a tangible model for earthly fatherhood. All men should look to the man God chose to lead the Holy Family.

St. Joseph's Covenant Keepers is an informal international network of Christian men, under the patronage of St. Joseph, dedicated to strengthening the family by following the eight commitments of SJCK.

Our Eight Commitments

As St. Joseph's Covenant Keepers, we commit ourselves to:

1. Affirming Christ's Lordship Over Our Families
2. Following St. Joseph, the Loving Leader and Head of the Holy Family
3. Loving Our Wives All Our Lives
4. Turning Our Hearts Toward Our Children
5. Educating Our Children in the Discipline and Instruction of the Lord
6. Protecting Our Families
7. Providing for Our Families
8. Building Our Marriages and Families on the "Rock"

These commitments are the basis for a growing movement of Christian fathers that seeks to transform the greater society through the transformation of families.

Calling All Fathers

The primary thrust of St. Joseph's Covenant Keepers (SJCK) is to men who are fathers of children still living at home. However, we warmly welcome Christian men of all ages, callings, and states in life: grandfathers wanting to strengthen their children and grandchildren; single men preparing for the vocation of marriage; and especially pastors serving as indispensable spiritual fathers[6] in the family of God. Participation is open to all men who agree with, and who are willing to promote, the eight commitments explained in chapters three through ten.

We do not want SJCK to be a top-heavy organization that becomes a focus and activity center for men. Our explicit desire is for men to focus on their own families. We believe that the family is vastly superior to any organization in its ability to renew both Church and society. Therefore, any activities of SJCK in small men's groups, parish SJCK organizations, or regional and national rallies, will be for the purpose of equipping and encouraging men for more effective service *within* their families.

As St. Joseph's Covenant Keepers, we will show concern not just for our own families. We will also strive for a Christlike concern for the spiritual and material welfare of other families in our communities, in our parishes, and throughout the world.

Not Band-Aids, But a Genuine Cure

We are passing through a period of profound cultural decay that is affecting marriages, families, and especially children in ways unparalleled in recorded history. St. Joseph's Covenant Keepers wants to bring all the power of the historic Christian Faith to strengthen your home. Our goal is not to offer you superficial comfort or make you feel pleasant while your marriage and family quietly disintegrate. Our goal is to help you know and live the truths that will enable your family to survive and thrive well into the third millennium.

The eight commitments described in this book are not easy to follow. Following Christ in any area of life always involves the narrow road. The broad way only appears easy. In reality, it lures the unsuspecting down the path of heartache and overwhelming hardship. Watered-down attempts to prop up contemporary family life are doomed in the face of modern pressures against marriage and the family. The solution to the needs of today's family begins with a challenge to husbands and fathers to follow the high and holy calling of Christian fatherhood.

Commitment One:

Affirming Christ's Lordship Over Our Families

As the leaders of our families, we will explicitly acknowledge the social kingship of Christ over our families. Toward this end we will have a home enthronement of the Sacred Heart of Jesus that we renew annually. We believe that the enthronement of the Sacred Heart deepens family life by bringing about a greater love between the Heart of Jesus and the hearts of parents and children. To invite Christ's loving Lordship and presence in our family, we will seek to have daily family prayer and Scriptures read aloud in the home. At least weekly on the Lord's Day, our family will worship together and receive Christ in the Eucharist, the ultimate source of our family life and unity.

3

Affirming Christ's Lordship
Over Our Families

"...choose this day whom you will serve ... as for me and my
house, we will serve the LORD."

—Joshua 24:15

As a cold rain drizzled outside the huge meeting hall, the air inside
grew warm and thick with the breath of a thousand Halleluias! The
insistent hum of the rain reinforced the preacher's mesmerizing elo-
quence. Although the revival had reached its fourth hour, the
evangelist's voice could still boom to a fever-pitch as he challenged
all sinners present to come forward to the "anxious bench" and re-
pent. Amidst fainting and weeping, four hundred people came forward to give their lives to Jesus Christ. The year was 1830. The
preacher was the brilliant New York revivalist, Charles Finney.

In the aftermath of the Second Great Awakening (which began
about 1800), Charles Finney brought an estimated half-million people
to Christ, without the aid of today's technology and mass media.
Finney perfected the techniques of protracted meetings, pitched
emotional appeals, and altar calls. Unfortunately, Finney's fiery revival fizzled, resulting in spiritual burn-out and religious indiffer-
ence. Upstate New York, the center of Finney's revival, became known
as the "burnt-over" district, where only sects like the Mormons were
able to evangelize successfully.

Citing the growing Christian men's movement, an editorial in *The Wall Street Journal* claims that the U.S. is in the midst of a Fourth Great Awakening.[1] Christian men everywhere are enthusiastic about promoting men's ministry. But we must be careful not to substitute high emotions for authentic renewal. Men are quite right to be excited about the Holy Spirit working in their lives. However, we can't let our adrenaline overwhelm our prudence.

A Spiritual "Report Card"

How can we tell whether the current revival will lead to authentic renewal or to spiritual devastation? We need some sort of religious "report card" to evaluate any men's movement. Jesus says that those who abide in him will bear *lasting* fruit (John 15:16). The mark of a true revival is lasting renewal. Any revival that fizzles in a few years is a failure. An authentic men's ministry will continue for generations: "The father may die, and yet he is not dead, for he has left behind him one like himself..." (Sirach 30:4).

The Dead Sea or the Sea of Galilee?

Renewal movements resemble one of the two bodies of water in Israel. The sparkling waters of the Sea of Galilee teem with life, encircled by prosperous towns and fertile, green fields. By contrast, the Dead Sea lies at the bottom of a barren, brown wasteland, its stagnant waters empty and lifeless. What's the difference? The Sea of Galilee has both an inlet and an outlet: it sends on the life it receives. The Dead Sea has only an inlet: it engulfs and suffocates everything that enters it.

Renewal movements often fall into the trap of self-absorption. They can lose sight of the greater purpose for which God is pouring out his Spirit. Hoarding God's graces leads to spiritual stagnation and barrenness. Dispersing God's graces to others leads to spiritual growth and fruitfulness. Only by passing its blessings on to the family will a men's revival survive.

House-to-House Evangelism

First-century Christians evangelized from house to house. The Gospel was not proclaimed to individuals alone but to entire families:

"Believe in the Lord Jesus, and you will be saved, *you and your household*" (Acts 16:31; also Luke 19:9). This family-to-family evangelism could not be stopped by the Imperial Rome's hostile, pagan culture. Christians living in the twenty-first century need to rediscover this winning strategy of the first century.

As Christians we should have a strong expectation for the world to be restored through the family. Grace never destroys nature, but rather perfects it. Since the family is the basic, vital cell of all human society, we should expect grace to be exceptionally active in and through the family. Our Holy Father Pope John Paul II has repeatedly emphasized that "the future of the world and of the Church passes through the family."[2]

For this reason, the primary purpose of St. Joseph's Covenant Keepers is to equip and encourage men for their leadership role *within* their own families.

Home Enthronements of the Sacred Heart

The long-term direction of any movement is often permanently flavored by its start. The best way to establish a family focus for a men's ministry is to promote enthronements of Jesus' Sacred Heart in the home.

What is a home enthronement? It is a solemn act of recognizing the loving kingship of Christ in the Christian family. During an enthronement ceremony, the family places an image or picture of the Sacred Heart in a prominent place and consecrates itself to Jesus. A home enthronement formally recognizes Christ as the family's permanent King and Lord. By acknowledging the kingship of Christ in the basic unit of society, the family, this ceremony advances the kingship of Christ in the larger society, the world.

This devotion is more than simply placing a picture on a living room wall, then forgetting about it. By enthroning the Sacred Heart in the home, each member of the family testifies to his complete submission and devotion to his King. Jesus is invited to participate in all family affairs. He is asked to sanctify every detail of the home. This ceremony implies the family's intention to live a faithful Christian life, in obedience to the loving will of the Sacred Heart.

Ignoring the Kingship of Christ

Why is the social recognition of Christ's kingship over the family important? Jesus Christ is not just Lord of the human heart. He is the "Lord of Lords and King of Kings." He is the ruler of civil governments as much as he is the ruler of families and individuals. Today, Christ's kingship over public life has been completely forgotten. As rulers and judges neglect, scorn, and reject God's laws, rivers of blood from the slaughter of innocents fill the cup of divine judgment.

Countless Christians in the first centuries chose martyrdom rather than burn a pinch of incense before an image of Caesar. They willingly chose to be dismembered and devoured by wild beasts rather than acknowledge that Caesar was supreme Lord. With their lives, these martyrs testified that Christ's kingdom began with his first advent. Unfortunately, the fact that Christ has a kingdom during this present age is a foreign idea to millions of Christians today.

What about Catholics? Far too many Catholics have never heard that Christ is the King of the world. The best Catholic summary on Christ's social kingship is found in Pope Pius XI's priceless encyclical, *On the Kingship of Christ*.[3]

In this encyclical, Pope Pius XI reminds all Christians:

> it is a dogma of faith that Jesus Christ was given to man, not only as our Redeemer, but also as a lawgiver, to whom obedience is due.... It would be a grave error, on the other hand, to say that Christ has no authority whatever in civil affairs.... Nor is there any difference in this matter between the individual and the family or the State; for all men, whether individually or collectively, are under the dominion of Christ.

What are the consequences of ignoring the social kingship of Christ? *On the Kingship of Christ* continues:

> men and nations cut off from God are stirring up strife and discord and hurrying along the road to ruin and death.... The result is that human society is tottering to its fall, because it has no longer a secure and solid foundation ... the unity and stability of the family is undermined.

Considering that he wrote this document in 1925, Pope Pius XI accurately prophesied the course of the twentieth century.

Restoring the Kingship of Christ

How do we restore the social kingship of Christ? Pope Pius XI first established the Feast of Christ the King. He also recommended Eucharistic exposition and processions and, finally, home and national enthronements of the Sacred Heart. "The kingship and empire of Christ have been recognized in the pious custom, practiced by many families, of dedicating themselves to the Sacred Heart of Jesus; not only families; but nations too, have performed the act of this dedication."[4]

It may be a long time until the nations regain their sanity and again acknowledge the social kingship of Christ. Does this mean that Christ's social kingship is to remain in eclipse until then? Not at all. We must remember that the family is the most basic cell of society. Christ's kingdom will advance by conquering one family at a time.

Encouraging Spiritual Leadership

The prophet Malachi highlights the irreplaceable role of fathers in the renewal of the faith, the family, and society. "And he will turn the hearts of fathers to their children and the hearts of children to their fathers" (Malachi 4:6). Fathers need support to assume their role as their family's spiritual leader.

Fathering does not come to men as naturally as mothering comes to women. "Due to the marginality of males in the reproductive process, fathering is a cultural acquisition to an extent that mothering is not. Hence, when a culture ceases to support a father's involvement with his own children (through its laws, mores, symbols, models, rituals) powerful natural forces take over in favor of the mother-alone family."[5] Home-based spiritual traditions encourage fathers to become home-based spiritual leaders.

Old Testament fathers led their families in the annual Passover celebration in the home. How can Christian men recover that same spiritual leadership today? One way is for a father to lead his family in a home enthronement and its annual renewal.

Limiting Domestic Tyranny

Home enthronements also provide a necessary check for the abuse of spiritual leadership. Since the fall into original sin, men are prone to abuse their leadership in the family in one of two ways: either by neglecting their families or by becoming domestic tyrants. Both are home-wreckers. The cure for domestic tyranny is *not* denying the spiritual leadership of fathers. This only encourages neglect, which will be fatal to the family. To cure the problem of domestic tyranny we must properly diagnose its cause.

A tyrant doesn't acknowledge any authority greater than himself. When husbands and fathers don't recognize a higher authority, they might be tempted to act as if their own will is supreme. But when a father enthrones Christ as Lord of the family, he places his power in Christ's service. The merciful reign of Christ's Sacred Heart deposes domestic tyranny.

Why Worship the Sacred Heart of Jesus?

Why should Christians adore the Sacred Heart of Jesus? The essence of this devotion is worshipping the love of God which led him to suffer and die for our sins. Many people are surprised to learn that this powerful devotion goes all the way back through Christian history to the Church Fathers and Divine Revelation itself. It did not originate with the private revelations given to St. Margaret Mary in France (1673-1675), although these certainly helped popularize and shape this ancient devotion.

While in recent times devotion to the Sacred Heart has been downplayed as unnecessary and outdated, or even ridiculed as superstitious and sentimental, every pope since Clement XIII (1765) has exhorted Christians to adore Jesus in His Sacred Heart. This devotion is beautifully explained in Pope Pius XII's encyclical, *On Devotion to the Sacred Heart*.[6]

But why adore Jesus through the image of his heart? The heart is rich in symbolism. It is the universal sign of love. All cultures have used the heart as the natural expression of love because the heart is very sensitive to human emotions. Anger, fear, and excitement immediately affect the heartbeat. Thus, the heart is naturally considered the seat of human emotions and the natural symbol of the will. Moreover, the heart is also the natural symbol of life. The heart pumps life-giving blood to the rest of the body. In the devotion to the Sacred Heart we meditate on the life-giving aspect of divine love.

Not surprisingly, God himself uses the symbol of the heart extensively in the Scriptures. In the Old Testament, God commands the Israelites to love him with all their hearts (Deuteronomy 6:5). God speaks figuratively of his heart being grieved (Genesis 6:6) and overwhelmed with pity (Hosea 11:8).

In the New Testament, with the Incarnation of Jesus, God Himself assumes a complete human nature. It was a real human heart that was pierced on Calvary (John 19:34) to become the source of all the sacraments. "From His wounded side flowed blood and water, the fountain of sacramental life in the Church. To his open heart the Savior invites all men, to draw water in joy from the springs of salvation."[7]

Union of Human Heart and Divine Person

No Christian questions worshipping the infinite love of God, which is the essence of this devotion. However, some Christians have questioned adoring Jesus' *human* heart. We must remember that Jesus is both God and man. Jesus' human heart is united to his divine person and is thus worthy of worship. As Pius XII put it, "His human heart, as the noblest part of human nature, is hypostatically united to the Person of the divine Word and must therefore be adored in the same way in which the Church adores the Person of the Incarnate Son of God."[8]

In our worship we focus on the human heart of Jesus because it symbolizes the infinite love of our Lord and Savior. "There is nothing, then, which forbids us to adore the most Sacred Heart of Jesus, since it participates in and is the natural and most expressive symbol of that inexhaustible love with which our divine Redeemer still loves mankind."[9]

As Pius XII wrote in *On Devotion to the Sacred Heart*: "In the face of so many evils which today more than ever disturb individuals, homes, nations, and the whole world, where, venerable brothers, is a remedy to be sought? Is there a devotion more excellent than that to the Sacred Heart of Jesus, one which is more in accord with the real nature of the Catholic faith or which better meets the needs of the Church and the human race today? What act of religion is nobler, more suitable, sweeter and more conducive to salvation, since this devotion is wholly directed to the love of God Himself?"

Jesus taught that our greatest obligation is to adore God with our whole heart, soul, mind, and strength. Devotion to the Sacred Heart directs us to God's infinite love for us and invites us to adore him, to thank him, and to spend our lives imitating him in return. No wonder recent popes have called this devotion, "a perfect profession of the Christian religion." It is certainly an ideal way to bring our families under the loving Lordship of Jesus Christ.[10] It is also an excellent way to inaugurate a men's ministry that will concentrate on restoring the family.

Building a Lasting Revival, One Family at a Time

Promoting home enthronements is the place to begin a men's apostolate. Start with a home enthronement campaign at least twice a year. Spend time educating and preparing men to have home enthronements either on the Feast of the Sacred Heart in June, or on the Feast of Christ the King in November.[11] Invite other families to your home enthronement to spark an interest in having their own. There are many more complicated, expensive, and even exciting ways to begin a men's revival, but none are more lasting and effective. As Christian men, we have confessed that Jesus Christ is Lord of our lives and Lord of all. Isn't it time that we publicly confess that Jesus Christ is Lord of our families as well?

Jesus solemnly warned that, "because wickedness is multiplied, most men's love will grow cold" (Matthew 24:12). The twentieth century has seen an unprecedented multiplication of wickedness. Just as Jesus warned, we have witnessed the tragic fruit of wickedness: love growing cold. When love freezes, families fracture by the millions. The family-based devotion to the Sacred Heart is a special provision to keep the fires of divine charity burning in our families even though we live in a culture that turns love to ice.

The day is past when a lukewarm and middle-of-the-road Christian commitment will sustain the faith or the family. Joshua, one of the great leaders of God's people in the Old Testament, challenged the Israelites to make a deliberate choice to follow God in faith, love, and obedience. Joshua publicly committed his family to God's authority. The challenging words of this father in the Old Testament reverberate through the centuries to fathers today: "choose this day whom you will serve ... as for me and my house, we will serve the LORD" (Joshua 24:15).

Commitment Two:

Following St. Joseph, the Loving Leader and Head of the Holy Family

St. Joseph, after the Blessed Virgin Mary, is the greatest of all saints in heaven. God chose him to be the husband of the Blessed Virgin Mary and the father of Jesus Christ in the fullest sense, except for physical generation. We will seek his intercession to fulfill our calling of leading our families to be like the Holy Family.

As husbands and fathers, we commit ourselves to be loving leaders and heads of our families following the examples of St. Joseph in serving the Holy Family, and Christ's humble service to the Church, his mystical bride. We will neither irresponsibly abandon our leadership role within our families, nor abuse our leadership role through sinful domination and domestic tyranny. Along with affirming the headship of husbands and fathers in a family, we simultaneously affirm the perfect and complete equality between husbands and wives.

Following St. Joseph, the Loving Leader and Head of the Holy Family

"If the foundations are destroyed, what can the righteous do?"

—Psalm 11:3

Blinded by a sudden spring squall on May 9, 1980, a wayward freighter slammed into a foundation piling of Florida's Sunshine Skyway. The force of the collision knocked a 1,200-foot center section of the bridge into Tampa Bay. Because of the low visibility, some unsuspecting motorists sped right off the Skyway and plummeted 150 feet to their deaths. Eyewitnesses gaped in horror as a Greyhound bus plunged off the bridge, killing everyone but the driver. A total of thirty-five people died in one of the worst bridge disasters in U.S. history.

Collapsing the Foundation of the Family

How serious is it when the leadership role of fathers is denied or neglected? For families, it is like the collapse of the center span of the Skyway bridge. It is impossible for the family to survive without all of its foundations. That is why Pope Pius XI said that if the irreplaceable roles of husbands and wives are undermined the family is in "proximate danger of ruin."[1]

We are seeing radical changes in Catholic and Christian families as they abandon the historic roles of husbands and wives. In 1960 a very popular Catholic fathering book appeared with the title, *The Head of the Family*. When the publishers reprinted the book in 1990, they changed the title to *The Father of the Family*.[2] The publishers explained that the majority of Catholic families now have a two-headed family structure, with mothers and fathers both sharing the headship. Until recently, a two-headed family, like a two-headed creature, was regarded as a monstrosity. The abnormal has now become the norm.

St. Paul's teaching on the husband's headship and the wife's obedience to her husband in Ephesians 5 and Colossians 3 has been removed from the Irish lexionary. In God's plan, a husband's leading and loving are a part of an indivisible whole. When churches quit proclaiming the husband's leadership role, husbands will start abandoning their wives and children. The Church and civil society need to explicitly encourage and support the husband's role in the family. Without a father, family life collapses. Gigantic family troubles are coming to the Emerald Isles and to those who vainly imagine that they can alter the fundamental structure of the family.

Changing a book's title and censoring the lexionary are just two examples of the massive erosion of Catholic family structure. Never before have Catholic families tried to exist without a principal authority. Families following this cultural course are in uncharted waters with danger ahead. The psalmist asks, "If the foundations are destroyed, what can the righteous do?" (Psalm 11:3). Not much. If a central pillar for family life is smashed, no amount of "fix-the-family" campaigns and family life sloganeering will repair the ruin that must certainly follow.

Building on Reality

Foundations are important. The modern agenda to eradicate the divinely established roles of husbands and wives is steaming towards the central pillar of the family. If its course continues unchecked, it will sink the contemporary family. Academic and government institutions can survive for decades on myths and fables. But every family, like every bridge, can only be built on reality.

St. Joseph's headship in the Holy Family is distasteful for those wishing to create a brave new world. Christless utopias and headless families are doomed to a humiliating failure. Ask the builders of Babel. They built on a base of vain imaginations. It simply doesn't work. Reality is the only firm foundation for a family, or for a Christian civilization. The loving leadership role of a husband and father never becomes obsolete. Tragically, what will become obsolete are the families who abandon solid foundations for those created out of thin air.

The Christian Concept of Headship

The New Testament teaches two truths regarding the covenant relationship of husbands and wives. The first truth is that there is perfect and complete equality between them. The second truth is that husbands are called to be *servant leaders* within their families. The term for this role is "headship."[4] We must hold both truths simultaneously for a balanced view of the family.

It is difficult for many people to keep two seemingly contradictory ideas in their minds at one time. The major heresies in the early Church over the identity of Christ arose from the tendency to separate complementary (mutually supporting) truths into "either-or" categories. Some ancient theologians did such a good job of emphasizing Christ's divinity that they denied or minimized his humanity. Others emphasized his humanity to the point of eclipsing his deity. It is easy to pit one position against the other, to say that Jesus is *either* God *or* man. It is hard to keep in our minds the truth that Jesus is *both* fully God *and* fully man. We can't overemphasize one aspect and neglect the other. We must combine both truths in balance.

The moment we say "headship" in contemporary society people hastily assume we are talking about male domination and female inferiority. Nothing could be further from the truth. Yet these reactions highlight the need to carefully define terms. As St. Joseph's Covenant Keepers we expressly define a husband's headship as **the type of loving leadership exhibited by St. Joseph in serving the Blessed Virgin Mary and Jesus in the Holy Family**. We are not talking about being a domestic tyrant or a domineering husband. Rather, we are talking about imitating both St. Joseph in his service to the Holy Family and Jesus in his service to his mystical bride, the Church. Both Jesus and St. Joseph demonstrate that Christian leadership is not a selfish exercise of power and domination.

Mutual Love and Complementary Roles

Pope Leo XIII in his timeless encyclical, *Christian Marriage*, emphasizes that mutual love must guide the complementary roles of husband and wife.

> ...the mutual duties of husband and wife have been defined, and their several rights accurately established. They are bound, namely, to have such feelings for one another as to cherish always very great mutual love, to be ever faithful to their marriage vow, and to give one another an unfailing and unselfish help. The husband is the chief of the family and the head of the wife. The woman, because she is flesh of his flesh, and bone of his bone, must be subject to her husband and obey him; not, indeed, as a servant, but as a companion, so that her obedience shall be wanting in neither honor nor dignity. Since the husband represents Christ, and since the wife represents the Church, let there always be, both in him who commands and in her who obeys, a heaven-born love guiding both in their respective duties. For *the husband is the head of the wife; as Christ is the head of the Church....Therefore, as the Church is subject to Christ, so also lets wives be to their husbands in all things* (Ephesians 5:23-24).[6]

Affirming Roles and Assuming Responsibilities

Most men are reluctant to assume the headship of their families. They will seldom shoulder their spiritual duties if they never hear that God expects them to do so. They need affirmation and encouragement to take up their God-given roles and responsibilities.

How do wives react to the idea of their husbands becoming the family leader? Most wives are tired of being responsible for everything. They *want* help in the home, especially from their husbands. But if the husband's leadership is seen as a license for domestic tyranny, then most wives are rightly going to oppose the idea. If, on the other hand, the husband's spiritual headship is seen as loving servant leadership, then most wives embrace the idea. No wife wants an Archie Bunker-clone for a husband. But almost every wife would love to have a man doing his best to follow the example of St. Joseph. This is why St. Joseph's Covenant Keepers is receiving such strong support from wives. Who wouldn't want to have a man around the house who is at least trying to imitate St. Joseph?

The real source of our modern agitation over Christian headship stems from a distorted idea of leadership. Christian leadership isn't a selfish exercise of power over others. Rather, it is a call to greater service towards those we lead.

> *A dispute also arose among them, which of them was to be regarded as the greatest. And he said to them, "The kings of the Gentiles exercise lordship over them; and those in authority over them are called benefactors. But not so with you; rather let the greatest among you become as the youngest, and the leader as one who serves..."* (Luke 22:24-26).

The Head of the Holy Family

Pope Benedict XV (1920) referred to St. Joseph as "the august *head* of the Holy Family." Pope Pius XI (1937) called him the "tender and vigilant *head* of the Holy Family." Pope Leo XIII (1892) observed: "[Here] all men were to behold the perfect exemplar [example] of domestic society.... In Joseph *heads* of the household are blessed with the unsurpassed model of fatherly watchfulness and care."[7] Pope John Paul II said in his Letter to Families (1994) that the Holy Family is to be "an icon and model of every human family."[8] Husbands, wives, and children need concrete models for roles within family life.

St. Joseph is the perfect model of a husband serving his family as a loving leader. Yet in some respects, the members of the Holy Family were not equal. The child of the family was the creator of the universe, the second person of the Blessed Trinity, the King of Kings and Lord of Lords. The mother was the most exalted human being ever created. Despite the unparalleled roles of mother and child, St. Joseph remained the head of the Holy Family.

When the angel Gabriel came from heaven to warn the Holy Family of Herod's pending attack, to whom did the angel give the message? Did he warn Jesus, the God-man and the Messiah? Did he alert Mary, the creature with the highest state of grace and perfection? The angel came to St. Joseph, not because he was greater than

Mary or Jesus, but because he was the husband and father. He was responsible for guarding the Holy Family. Christian headship refers to service in a God-given role. It is a huge mistake to confuse it with a selfish quest for superiority or domination.

Is Headship Outdated?

Is the model of the father as the head of the family outdated? Are fathers in the third millennium different from fathers in the 1950s? Pope Pius XI in his encyclical, *On Christian Marriage*, gave a timeless answer to this question. His teaching will keep contemporary family life from going overboard in one of two harmful directions.

Pope Pius XI first asserts the headship of the husband. He then balances this statement with an affirmation of the liberty and dignity of the woman in her role as wife and mother. He says that the wife is *not* obligated to "obey her husband's every request if not in harmony with right reason or with the dignity due to [the] wife." Pope Pius immediately follows by insisting that proper headship "forbids that exaggerated liberty which cares not for the good of the family; it forbids that in this body which is the family, the heart be separated from the head to the great detriment of the whole body and the proximate danger of ruin. For if *the man is the head, the woman is the heart*, and as he occupies the chief place in ruling, so she may and ought to claim for herself the chief place in love."[9]

Pius XII proclaims that this basic structure of the family is unchangeable, while acknowledging that this permanent pattern will find varying expressions. "Again, this subjection of wife to husband in its degree and manner may vary according to the different condition of persons, place, and time.... **But the structure of the family and its fundamental law, established and confirmed by God, must always and everywhere be maintained intact.**"[10]

Will the role of a husband and father in the third millennium look different from that of the 1950s? Obviously it will. However, we can't change the fundamental roles of the husband as the head and the wife as the heart of the family because they are established by God. If we alter the basic, God-given structure of the family we will destroy it.

The Joyful Dance

Christian writer Thomas Howard compares universal reality to a joyful dance in which all creation is invited to participate:

> This notion of moral fixity seems repressive to moderns. What we need, we say, for our authentic freedom, is spontaneity, functionalism, and self-determination. But … paradoxically, we grow into our real selfhood and liberty by learning the steps in the Dance. The Dance is there. It is already choreographed. The music is playing. All creatures—all stars, all archangels, all lions and eagles and oak trees and seas and clams and grasshoppers—are dancing. The great thing is to learn the steps appointed for you and to move into your place.[11]

We discover meaning, purpose, and fulfillment by entering the dance and engaging in our God-given roles. In the dance called marriage, one leads, one follows, as the two move in joyous harmony. Contrast this to modern "dance" where men and women engage in independent, self-absorbed, inharmonious gyrations. Both lead, no one follows, and the very concept of harmony dies.

The tragic price modern selfhood exacts from marriage is a profound loss of joy. In the wake of this loss, therapists rush in and tell us to focus more on ourselves. Unfortunately, the rabid pursuit of self-esteem, self-fulfillment, and self-discovery will only leave men and women more empty, more alone, and even more joyless.

Joyful marriages and healthy families result, not from relational novelties, but from following the time-tested divine pattern. Men and women have different but complementary roles in their mutual service within the family. It is not for us to re-invent the eternal dance, but to joyfully participate in it.

Returning to Traditional Roles?

Already, secular researchers seem more sensitive than their Catholic counterparts to the critical need for fathers in families.[12] Ironically, secularists may well rediscover the essential leadership role of husbands before Christians do. In the meantime, the future of the family will be best served by a careful reexamination of the historical Christian record along with a diligent study of the best classical and contemporary research.[13]

Twenty more years of following today's norms will destroy the family. Like the Church and the state, the family needs a clearly defined leadership structure to survive. Take away the authority structure in any of these social units and the result will resemble the catastrophic collapse of the Sunshine Skyway.

Rediscovering the World's Greatest Father

As men rediscover the historic Christian roles of husbands and fathers, they will ultimately rediscover the importance of St. Joseph for both our churches and our homes. There is a connection between our "fatherless America" and our "fatherless churches." St. Joseph used to be an integral figure in most Catholic sanctuaries. In many of the newer Catholic churches, St. Joseph has disappeared. We need his return.

What role will St. Joseph play in the restoration of fatherhood? For centuries, Catholic spiritual writers have said that St. Joseph will be a great leader in the latter days of the Church. They knew that St. Joseph, like the patriarch Joseph in Genesis, would remain hidden in God's providence until the appointed time. Father Isidore Isolano, a sixteenth-century Dominican priest, wrote: "We have every reason to believe that the immortal God wishes at the end of time to honor St. Joseph in the empire of the Church Militant with honors most brilliant, and to render him the object of most profound veneration."[14]

The contemporary men's movement needs St. Joseph. Abstract principles, promises, and commitments are not enough to bring about deep personal change. What we need in this age of crisis in fatherhood is an ideal man to be a tangible model of Christian fatherhood. Where will we find such an exemplar? Let's look where Mary and Jesus looked: to St. Joseph.

How can we expect the Christian men's movement to succeed without St. Joseph? He is unquestionably the world's greatest father. By God's design, St. Joseph should be at the center of fatherhood's restoration. Our families will experience genuine and lasting renewal to the degree they imitate the Holy Family. Christian fathers will succeed to the degree they emulate St. Joseph.

To discover why he is the world's greatest father, we need to explore three key relationships in St. Joseph's life: his relationship with Mary, with Jesus, and with the Heavenly Father.

St. Joseph's Relationship with Mary

St. Joseph was not the biological father of Jesus, yet Holy Scripture and the Mother of our Lord call him Jesus' father (Luke 2:48). Why?

Fatherhood is rooted in the marriage covenant. St. Joseph's paternity springs entirely out of his marriage covenant with the Blessed Virgin Mary. Christian and Jewish theologians recognize that Joseph and Mary were legally married at their betrothal. Thus, Joseph and Mary were bonded in the marriage covenant at the time of the Annunciation.

St. Joseph is more than an "adoptive" father of Jesus. An adoptive father receives a child born *outside* of the marriage covenant. Jesus' conception and birth were *within* the marriage covenant. Thus Joseph was the father of Jesus in every way, except biologically.

The essence of St. Joseph's fatherhood, like all Christian fatherhood, grows out of the marriage covenant. Breaking the marriage covenant between Joseph and Mary would have eliminated the basis of St. Joseph's fatherhood. Divorce doesn't just destroy the marriage covenant, it destroys fatherhood.[15] When fatherhood collapses, families fracture and cultures decay. Ignoring the problem of husbands breaking their marriage covenants may make them feel better in the short run, but it will abort any long-term success of the Christian men's movement.

St. Joseph's Relationship with Jesus

The profound oneness created by the covenant of marriage includes the complete and total sharing of goods. "For marriage is the most intimate of all unions which from its essence imparts a community of gifts between those that by it are joined together."[16] St. Joseph shared with the Blessed Virgin both her unique graces and the supreme good given to their marriage, namely the child Jesus.

Joseph is the father: his fatherhood is not one that derives from begetting offspring; but neither is it an 'apparent' or merely 'substitute fatherhood.' Rather, it is one that fully shares in authentic human fatherhood and the mission of a father in a family.[17]

It was the ancient Jewish custom for fathers to name their children. The Jewish people did not choose names lightly. Names had great significance and meaning. St. Joseph received a divine command to name the child "Jesus" (Matthew 1:21). "In conferring the name, Joseph declares his own legal fatherhood over Jesus, and in speaking the name he proclaims the child's mission as Savior."[18]

As members of the New Covenant family of God, Jesus calls us "brothers" (Hebrews 2:11-13). If Jesus is our brother, then we have both an earthly father and a heavenly Father in the throne room of the universe. We all have a tendency to underestimate the richness of the inheritance Christ shares with us in the New Covenant. Do we realize that we have an exalted earthly father in heaven who cares for us as much as he cared for Jesus in Bethlehem, Egypt, and the carpenter shop in Nazareth?[19]

To the thousands of men deprived of a healthy relationship with their fathers: Go to St. Joseph! To those seeking to overcome a negative father image: Go to St. Joseph! To the millions of children in fatherless families: Go to St. Joseph! You will find an earthly father who, like the heavenly Father, is a father to the fatherless. The heavenly Father has provided a link to himself through the fatherhood of St. Joseph over the whole family of God.

St. Joseph's Relationship with the Heavenly Father

Like every father, Joseph was called to be a living image of the heavenly Father to his child. Any father contemplating this high calling might be tempted to despair because of his personal inadequacies. However, God always provides the grace to fulfill his commands. The calling to fatherhood is no exception.

God gave St. Joseph the heart of a father.

The same hand which forms each of the hearts of men makes the heart of a father in Joseph and the heart of a son in Jesus.... The true Father of Jesus Christ ... having chosen holy Joseph to act as the father of His Son in time has in a certain fashion infused a ray or spark of the infinite love which He bears His Son. This changes Joseph's heart, and gives him the love of a father.[20]

God plans to do extraordinary things in the lives of ordinary men. Our problem is that our expectations of what God wants to accomplish through us as fathers are too small. Centuries ago the prophet Malachi (4:5-6) told us to expect a miraculous transformation in the hearts of fathers and their children. Can we dare to believe that God wants to place within us the heart of a father as he did to St. Joseph?

A Prayer to Receive the Heart of a Father

For this reason I bow my knees before the Father, from whom every family in heaven and on earth is named, that according to the riches of his glory he may grant you to be strengthened with might through his Spirit in the inner man, and that Christ may dwell in your hearts through faith; that you, being rooted and grounded in love, may have power to comprehend with all the saints what is the breadth and length and height and depth, and to know the love of Christ which surpasses knowledge, that you may be filled with all the fulness of God. Now to him who by the power at work within us is able to do far more abundantly than all that we ask or think, to him be glory in the church and in Christ Jesus to all generations, for ever and ever. Amen (Ephesians 3:14-21).

φφφ 74:59

Commitment Three:

Loving Our Wives All Our Lives

As covenant keepers, we believe that a lawful Christian marriage is indissoluble. We believe that the sacrament of marriage is a lifelong covenant bond made possible by the abundant graces available in the New Covenant. We do not believe that marriage is a breakable contract. The indissolubility of the marriage covenant is the foundation for marriage and for the future of the family. As fathers, we realize the greatest gift we can ever give our children is faithfulness to our marriage vows. We believe that a willful divorce from a lawful marriage is covenant breaking in the most profound sense. If problems arise within our marriages we will seek help to heal our marriages and not seek a divorce. We will help others with whom we are networked to do the same. We will also take steps to keep our marriages strong, even when serious marital problems are absent. To help maintain lifelong covenant faithfulness to our wives, we will avoid both the remote and near occasions that may lead to the sin of adultery.

5

Loving Our Wives All Our Lives

"Husbands, love your wives, as Christ loved the church and gave himself up for her...."

—Ephesians 5:25

"The Eucharist is the very source of Christian marriage. ...the Eucharist is a fountain of charity."

—*The Role of the Christian Family in the Modern World*, section 57

It's a familiar story: Sam and Irene fall in love and get married. They expect the rest of their lives to be something like an extended honeymoon when suddenly they find themselves in a replay of *Star Wars*. They can't seem to agree on even the simplest things. Cute little quirks have become major irritations. Sam loved Irene for being helpless, but now he's frustrated that she can't fix anything. Irene loved Sam for being the "strong, silent type," but now she's upset that he can't share his feelings. Sam was a friendly guy who got along with everybody. Irene was a congenial person who never had an enemy in her life. These two likable people got married, hoping to live happily ever after. Now there is an interstellar battle of the wills going on under the roof of their three-bedroom, two-bath home. All too often, this tale describes the everyday struggles of our own marriages.

Deep in our hearts we know that this is not the way marriage is supposed to be. When marriage difficulties arise, we might start to wonder if we really married the right person. We might be tempted to get a divorce, to start over with someone new and seemingly more compatible. But those who abandon their first spouse for another inevitably find the same frustrations they just left.

Raising the Standard in Our Marriages

The solution to marriage problems is not a new spouse, but rather a new standard of love. St. Paul calls us to love our wives as Christ loves the Church. "Husbands, love your wives, as Christ loved the church and gave himself up for her..." (Ephesians 5:25). Let's be honest: does any of us truly love our wives as Christ loves his Church? If all husbands had a Christlike love for their wives, there would be very little marital strife and even less divorce. Above all, wives want their husbands' unconditional love. As husbands, we truly *want* to love our wives as they deserve. We would like to give our wives the kind of sacrificing, nourishing, cherishing love that Christ gives his Church. But so often we find this high standard impossible to achieve. Why do we find it so difficult to love our wives as we should?

A quick survey of the Bible reveals the answer. The Humpty Dumpty rhyme, slightly paraphrased, neatly summarizes the history of salvation and its corresponding effect upon marriage: *Humpty Dumpty sat on a wall*—the creation of Adam and Eve in Genesis 2; *Humpty Dumpty had a great fall*—the fall into original sin in Genesis 3; *and all the king's soldiers and all the marital therapists, along with all the self-help programs, couldn't put Humpty's marriage back together again*. Why not? Sin dealt marriage a near-fatal blow. Original sin hardened the human heart.

Throughout Scripture the marriage covenant parallels and reflects the divine covenant. The second chapter of Genesis uses God's covenant name, Yahweh, for the first time as God enters into a covenant with Adam and Eve. After describing the first divine covenant, this chapter goes on to describe the first marriage. As God and his people became one in the divine covenant, so Adam and Eve became one in the marriage covenant.

The third chapter of Genesis records the fall into original sin. In covenant terms this first sin was an act of covenant breaking. The fracturing of the divine covenant immediately caused a rift in the marriage covenant. In history's first marital squabble, Adam blames Eve for his own disobedience. The dual effects of original sin are: (a) a broken covenant with God; and (b) a crippling of the human heart's ability to love spouse and neighbor.

Sin is Spelled "s**I**n"

Isn't sin something we just talk about in church? What does sin have to do with marriage? To visualize what sin does to marriage imagine writing the word "sin" with a tiny "s," a tiny "n," and a huge, inflated "I" in the middle. Sin makes us selfish. Sin makes ego-maniacs out of otherwise nice, ordinary people. Trying to fit two centers of the universe in a three-bedroom home inevitably causes intergalactic friction. The scriptures teach that genuine love is a profound self-giving. This love, also known as charity, is the opposite of selfishness. Self-giving love is the essential ingredient for a happy marriage.

If too much "I" is the problem, more "I" cannot be the solution. Self-help and self-esteem programs can sometimes alleviate a few symptoms of the human condition, but they are incapable of curing the root problem of selfishness. While self-discovery might provide temporary relief for certain problems, it simultaneously strengthens the core problem of selfishness. Trying to overcome selfishness by focusing on self is like trying to pull our fingers out of a Chinese fingerlock. The harder we try, the more stuck we become. We have to look outside ourselves to heal the wounds sin inflicts on the human heart. We don't need self-help; we need divine help. Only the King's Son can put Humpty Dumpty and his marriage back together again. Only Christ can make the human heart capable of lifelong love.

The Old Covenant Promises a New Heart

The Old Covenant was incapable of washing away original sin and repairing hard hearts.[1] Therefore, the prophets spoke of a new covenant that would restore the human heart and make it capable of loving God and neighbor. In Jeremiah's prophecy of the New Covenant (chapter 31), God refers to himself as a husband to whom the people of Israel have been unfaithful. Just as in Genesis 2, the marriage covenant is a profound reflection of the divine covenant. The graces for both covenant keeping with God and covenant keeping in marriage were made available through the New Covenant.

"Behold, the days are coming, says the LORD, *when I will make a new covenant with the house of Israel and the house of Judah, not like the covenant which I made with their fathers when I took them by the hand to bring them out of the land of Egypt, my covenant which they broke, though I was their husband, says the* LORD. *But this is the covenant which I will make with the house of Israel after those days, says the* LORD: *I will put my law within them, and I will write it upon their hearts; and I will be their God, and they shall be my people"* (Jeremiah 31:31-33).

Ezekiel's prophecy of the New Covenant promises nothing less than a new heart. The Messiah, that is the Christ, will restore God's people to a profound oneness with the Heavenly Father never dreamed of in the Old Covenant.

"A new heart I will give you, and a new spirit I will put within you; and I will take out of your flesh the heart of stone and give you a heart of flesh. And I will put my spirit within you, and cause you to walk in my statutes and be careful to observe my ordinances" (Ezekiel 36:26-27).

The New Covenant Transforms Marriages

The deepest effects of this New Covenant restoration with God would be especially present in the marriage covenant. Jesus deliberately began his three-year New Covenant ministry while attending a wedding feast in Cana (John 2). During the wedding ceremony the hosts ran out of wine. This was a supreme embarrassment at a Jewish wedding. Nearby were six large water pots each containing twenty- to thirty-gallons of water used in Jewish ceremonial washings. Jesus miraculously changed this water into the finest wine.

In a small town like Cana, one hundred twenty to one hundred eighty gallons of extra wine was far more than would be needed to get everyone at the wedding feast completely loaded. What is being signified through this first miracle of Jesus' public ministry? Is the main point simply that Jesus wants us to have a good time at wedding receptions? Or is there something more significant in this miracle? The water in the pots was used for Old Testament ceremonial washings. These external washings were incapable of repairing sin's damage to the human heart.

Superabundant Graces for Marriage

This first miracle in the New Testament teaches us that a transformation will take place in the New Covenant. The grace that was lacking in the Old Testament will be found in abundance in the New. Where there was selfishness now there will be gallons upon gallons of charity available. The good news for married couples is that the marriage covenant would be a chief beneficiary of these graces.

> The Church attaches great importance to Jesus' presence at the wedding at Cana. She sees in it the confirmation of the goodness of marriage and the proclamation that thenceforth marriage will be an efficacious sign of Christ's presence. The matrimonial covenant ... between baptized persons has been raised by Christ the Lord to the dignity of a sacrament.[2]

The sacrament of Matrimony gives spouses the graces to fulfill their lifelong vows as covenant keepers.

Where Do We Get These Superabundant Graces?

How do we receive these gallons of New Testament graces signified by the new wine at Cana? This same Gospel gives us the answer.

Chapters 13 through 17 of John's Gospel contain teachings of Jesus that are unique in the New Testament. In these priceless chapters, St. John gives us Christ's discourse while he was in the upper room with his disciples instituting the Eucharist during the Last Supper. St. John had his head resting upon the heart of Jesus during the Last Supper, an indication of his special closeness to Christ. St. John plumbs the depths of what it means to live a Eucharistic life with Christ. The Eucharistic implications for marriage are staggering.

During the Last Supper Christ declared:

> *"I am the true vine, and my Father is the vinedresser. Every branch of mine that bears no fruit, he takes away, and every branch that does bear fruit he prunes, that it may bear more fruit. You are already made clean by the word which I have spoken to you. Abide in me, and I in you. As the branch cannot bear fruit by itself, unless it abides in the vine, neither can you, unless you*

abide in me. I am the vine, you are the branches. He who abides in me, and I in him, he it is that bears much fruit, for apart from me you can do nothing. If a man does not abide in me, he is cast forth as a branch and withers; and the branches are gathered, thrown into the fire and burned. If you abide in me, and my words abide in you, ask whatever you will, and it shall be done for you. By this my Father is glorified, that you bear much fruit, and so prove to be my disciples. As the Father has loved me, so have I loved you; abide in my love" (John 15:1-9).

Abiding in Christ = Receiving His Body and Blood

How do we abide in Christ? When Christ commands us to remain in him, he is not just giving a general exhortation to maintain a spiritual union with him. Rather, Christ is describing a very specific way to live in him. Through his grapevine imagery Christ is commanding a Eucharistic indwelling. He solemnly warns that anything short of this will eventually result in a withering of the spiritual life. It is not enough to abide in a symbol of Jesus, an experience of Jesus, a thought of Jesus, or even in a spiritual presence of Jesus. To obtain the new wine of the New Covenant, we must literally abide in the body and blood of Jesus. The divine covenant creates a family-like bond between God and his people.

The Eucharist is the heart of the New Covenant where Christ the bridegroom actually becomes "one flesh" with his bride, the Church. Anything less than a Eucharistic abiding falls short of what it means to have a dynamic personal relationship with Jesus in the New Covenant.

True Love Is Impossible Without Christ

As husbands we will not merely find it difficult to love our wives as we should, we shall discover that it is impossible. Jesus is unmistakable on this point: "apart from me you can do nothing" (John 15:5). These words should strike terror in our self-reliant hearts. By our own efforts, we can never love our wives all our lives. Maintaining an indissoluble marriage filled with charity is humanly impossible.

Christ solemnly commands us to Eucharistically abide in him:

So Jesus said to them, "Truly, truly, I say to you, unless you eat the flesh of the Son of man and drink his blood, you have no life in you; he who eats my flesh and drinks my blood has eternal life, and I will raise him up at the last day. For my flesh is food indeed, and my blood is drink indeed. He who eats my flesh and drinks my blood abides in me, and I in him. As the living Father sent me, and I live because of the Father, so he who eats me will live because of me" (John 6:53-57).

Jesus promises that if we abide in him, we shall be able to "love one another" as he has loved us (John 15:12). Apart from Christ, we cannot love our wives as Christ has loved us. By abiding in Christ through the Eucharist, we will have superabundant graces available to transform our hearts and renew our marriages.

The Eucharist is the secret to transforming selfishness into love. The Eucharist is where we find Cana's gallons and gallons of New Covenant graces empowering our hearts to truly love. By abiding in the Eucharistic Christ, we will have the grace to love our wives as Christ loves us and to love our wives all our lives.

The Eucharist Is a Fountain of Charity!

Every marriage needs more love. In *The Role of the Christian Family in the Modern World*, Pope John Paul II says, "The Eucharist is the very source of Christian marriage.... In this sacrifice of the New and Eternal Covenant, Christian spouses encounter the source from which their own marriage covenant flows, is interiorly structured and continuously renewed. As a representation of Christ's sacrifice of love for the Church, *the Eucharist is a fountain of charity.*"[3]

Every home needs a fountain of charity overflowing within it, washing away selfishness and revitalizing the marriage covenant. The answer for hurting marriages is not divorce, but Christ. We need less of ourselves and more of Christ. We need God dwelling within our hearts and energizing our love. The Eucharist is the supernatural secret for making love last forever. The Eucharistic Christ is indissoluble superglue binding our marriages together for a lifetime of love.

Then Why Isn't There More Love?

Many spouses go to the sacrament of the Eucharist regularly and still have miserable marriages. People often receive Christ's body and blood without a "fountain of charity" overflowing in their hearts.

The Catholic divorce rate in the United States is close to the national average, which is the highest in the world. Why isn't the Eucharist transforming more marriages?

We tend to receive from God what we ask for with expectant faith. We often go to Mass without expecting to receive anything for our marriages. When was the last time we approached Christ in the Blessed Eucharist and asked him to give us the graces we need for our marriages? Amazingly, many Catholic couples have never linked in their minds, or in their prayers, the sacrament of Marriage with the sacrament of the Blessed Eucharist. If we approach Christ in the Eucharist with even the tiniest amount of faith and ask him to strengthen our marriages, we will find gallons of his love flooding our hearts.

Another obstacle to Eucharistic graces is a lack of forgiveness in our hearts. We can't expect Christ to fill us with his graces in the Eucharist if we ignore his commands in scripture to extend forgiveness, especially to our wives and children.[4] Unforgiveness in our hearts grieves the Holy Spirit and smothers God's grace within us. "So if you are offering your gift at the altar, and there remember that your brother has something against you, leave your gift there before the altar and go; first be reconciled to your brother, and then come and offer your gift" (Matthew 5:23-24). Before we approach the altar to receive our Lord Jesus, we need both to receive forgiveness from God and to extend forgiveness to others.

Finally, eating the "bread of life" won't help us if our souls are spiritually dead. Receiving the Eucharist in the state of serious sin is a common reason why this sacrament fails to transform hearts and marriages. Christ's life-giving grace is completely blocked if we are in the state of unforgiven mortal sin. Even the habit of committing less serious sins can constrict the channels of grace. The fault lies not in the power of the Eucharist, but in our sin-full souls. The grace of the sacrament can't reach us if our spiritual arteries are clogged by sin.

The Sacrament of Reconciliation

How do we unclog these spiritual arteries? By frequenting another important sacrament: Reconciliation. This sacrament of confession and forgiveness cleans out the hardened arteries of our heart: it pulverizes the plaque of pride, dissolves the fatty deposits of deceit, and strips away the scars of selfishness. A valid confession is spiritual open-the-heart surgery: all the clots of sin are removed and the heart receives a life-giving transfusion of Christ's grace.

Remember how we spelled "sin" with a huge, bloated "I"? All sin is the inflation of self, saying "my will" instead of "thy will" be done. Sin expresses and reinforces selfishness, the root of marital discord. The sacrament of Confession is the antidote to sin and selfishness. It takes humility to confess our particular sins to another man and ask him to extend Christ's forgiveness, even if Christ has appointed him for that purpose.[5] How much more would we rather just confess our sins generally and privately to God, preferably on some lonely hill in the dead of night? But the divine Physician made Reconciliation to be medicine for our souls. Nothing shrinks the ego like the humility of confessing particular faults. Nothing destroys selfishness like asking pardon from Christ through another human being. It certainly would be easier to ignore sin[6] and avoid the sacrament of Reconciliation, but it is more important to root out self-love and drink deeply of God's mercy.

Reconcile with Your Wife

Once we are reconciled with God, it is easier to reconcile with our wives. Having tasted God's merciful forgiveness, it is easier for us to extend forgiveness in return. This is a great time to do something many husbands rarely do: apologize. Men often use their wives as emotional punching bags, expressing their spiritual frustration in anger, nit-picking, and bitterness. Sin always comes out: either in confession or in screwball behavior. Confession is the time for divine mercy. After confession is the time for mutual mercy. Take the initiative and sincerely ask for your covenant partner's forgiveness and forgive her in the generous measure that God has forgiven you. Forgive and then forget, forever.

It's a great idea to take your whole family to the sacrament of Reconciliation. Afterward, it will be easy for all the family members to ask forgiveness from one another for any faults committed. (Be prepared for your children's shock and admiration when you ask them for *their* forgiveness!) Then, when we receive Christ's Body and Blood with an expectant faith and a clean conscience, there will be nothing to hinder God's grace from rushing into our souls and transforming our hearts, our marriages, and our families.

> There is no family that does not know how selfishness, discord, tension and conflict violently attack and at times mortally wound its own communion: hence there arise the many and varied forms of division in family life. But at the same time, every family is called by the God of peace to have the joyous and renewing experience of "reconciliation," that is, communion reestablished, unity restored. In particular, participation in the sacrament of Reconciliation and in the banquet of the one Body of Christ offers to the Christian family the grace and the responsibility of overcoming every division and of moving towards the fullness of communion willed by God, responding in this way to the ardent desire of the Lord: "that they may be one."[7]

Why Do We Need a Catholic Men's Movement?

I am often asked, "Why do we need a Catholic men's movement when our Protestant brothers are doing such a fine job already." My reply is: "Yes, they are doing an excellent job in reaching Christian men. However, both Protestant and Catholic men desperately need the fullness of the Catholic faith for three reasons: the sacrament of Marriage, the sacrament of Reconciliation, and the sacrament of the Blessed Eucharist."[8] Christ intends for each of these sacraments to be appreciated and practiced for marriage and family life to succeed in the New Covenant. The Catholic faith not only proclaims the highest standards for the indissolubility of marriage, but it also provides, through the sacraments, the best delivery system to achieve them.

All Christians need to realize that marriage is more than just a religious ordinance; it is one of the sacraments through which Christ promises to provide strengthening graces to married couples. Every Christian spouse needs the healing powers of the sacrament of Reconciliation and the gallons of charity that flow from the sacrament of the Blessed Eucharist. These three sacraments deliver special graces that Jesus intends for all Christian couples. Charity demands that we shout this good news for Christian marriages from the rooftops.

One Final Secret

Have you ever listened to children playing in a sandbox? If you go by a sandbox filled with four-year-old girls, what will you hear? Probably the sounds of chattering as the little girls engage each other in animated conversation. If you go by a sandbox filled with four-year-old boys, what will you hear? Probably the sounds of grunting and revving as the little boys push their trucks through the sand.

The verbal skills of four-year-old girls typically surpass those of four-year-old boys. Unfortunately for men, this lack of verbal expertise seems to follow us through life. We constantly lag behind women in our ability to communicate. This communication difference between men and women becomes even more pronounced in marriage.

You've probably heard that men are from Mars and women are from Venus. However, the problem is much worse than that. Women are indeed from Venus, but men are from deep outer space. How can men come back into orbit with their wives? The secret to the mutual planetary attraction of spouses is for men to learn how to communicate with their wives so that they aren't living, emotionally speaking, in another galaxy. This one little secret can transform a marriage almost overnight.

A healthy marriage is like a strong threefold cord.[9] It has three indispensable bonds: physical, spiritual, and emotional. Men generally focus on the physical bond, while women typically concentrate on the emotional. The emotional bond is nourished and strengthened by communication. For wives, verbal communication is one of the most significant ways husbands can show their love. At the same time, many husbands are nearly oblivious to the verbal needs of their wives. A wife will never feel truly fulfilled in marriage if her husband does not strengthen the emotional bond by communicating frequently. In stark contrast, a husband from outer space says to his wife, "I told you twenty years ago that I loved you and if I ever change my mind I'll let you know!"

The natural difference in communication styles between men and women is difficult for most husbands to overcome. Yet over the past thirty years, something else has aggravated this natural difference and caused men to be lost in space when it comes to communicating with their wives. It has become increasingly common for couples to have premarital sexual relations. Premarital sex weakens two of the three marital bonds. How?

When a couple has premarital sexual relations they know that they are breaking God's commandments. As a result, their spiritual bond is broken at the very time their spiritual relationship should be maturing.

Deep interpersonal communication takes place in all sexual relations. It is very easy for a man to feel like he is building the emotional bond with his wife-to-be during premarital sexual relations. A man often thinks that he is completely sharing his feelings in the sexual embrace: "Boy, are we ever communicating!" When a man starts having premarital sex, he stops developing his verbal communication skills. Physical bonding replaces emotional bonding. During the critically important months before marriage, a man should be learning how to express himself in non-physical ways to his fiancée. Instead, the intensity of the physical communication eclipses the verbal. The husband enters marriage with fast-frozen emotional skills. As a result, many marriages shatter.

In 1988 the average length of marriages in the U.S. that ended in divorce was seven years. Twenty percent of these divorcing couples ended their marriage before their third anniversary.[10] In the typical county courthouse in the U.S., the majority of the filings for the dissolution of marriage are made by women. This is surprising since women are usually working the hardest to hold a marriage together. What makes so many wives, after a few years of marriage, willing to throw in the towel?

A 1989 study done by the *National Survey of Families and Households* found that "unions begun by cohabitation are almost twice as likely to dissolve within ten years."[11] Another study reported in 1991 in the *Journal of Marriage and the Family* found that "nonvirgins have a divorce rate that is 53 percent to 71 percent higher than virgins."[12] A third study by the National Council on Family Relations found that newlyweds who had premarital relations were less happy and that the wives complained about poor communication after the wedding.[13]

All three of these studies confirm that premarital sex puts a huge (and unnecessary) stress upon a marriage. It shatters two of the three bonds of marriage. Not only does it sever the spiritual bond, but premarital sex also freezes a man's already puny communication skills. After enough years of emotional neglect, the wife finally feels frozen out. She marches down to the courthouse and files for divorce.

How do couples who have started their marriages on the wrong foot renew their spiritual and emotional bonds? First, honestly acknowledge that God knew what he was doing in commanding us to save the sexual embrace for marriage. God graciously gave Moses the prescription for lasting marriages three thousand years before our contemporary sociologists. Second, if the premarital relations have not been confessed, go to the sacrament of Reconciliation. Third, for spouses who have never developed their spiritual bond, begin to pray together. Fourth, for husbands who have allowed their verbal skills to lie dormant, start communicating with your wife. Put in a little extra effort to strengthen the emotional bond with your spouse. Husbands who have taken small but sincere steps to communicate their love and appreciation to their wives have almost miraculously transformed their marriages.

How well does this little effort at communication work? Our office received a long-distance call from Virginia on a Monday following one of our weekend St. Joseph's Covenant Keepers conferences. It seems that one of the Navy men attending the conference turned to his wife as he was leaving for duty on Monday morning and said something like, "I just want you to know that I am grateful you are my wife and that I love you." These simple words put a spark in the heart of this sailor's wife. She enthusiastically called her friends to share the excitement of her husband's declaration. Her friends called others including us at the Family Life Center. We were amazed to hear the joy created by twenty seconds of emotional communication.

After a men's conference in Cincinnati, another man decided to listen more carefully to his wife and to share not only his thoughts but also his feelings with her. When he told his wife of his resolve, she took him to see their marriage counselor. Previously, this couple had been near the brink of divorce and gone to marital therapy for years. After hearing the husband's intentions to communicate with his wife on a more sensitive level, the therapist acknowledged that they would no longer need his services. This demonstrates the incredible power of verbal communication to strengthen a marriage.

It only takes a few seconds, but this simple secret of communicating can literally transform your marriage. Take a few moments and tell your wife how much she means to you. Tell her why you married her and why you'd marry her again. Praise her for all she does to make your house a home. Thank her for being the mother of your children. Affirm how much richer she has made your life. Share your hopes and dreams. Pray with her, and pray *for* her. Ask her what she is thinking. And then really listen!

When it comes to loving our wives, men don't have to be in outer space. If we carefully build the spiritual, emotional, and physical bonds with our covenant partner, we will preserve a strong planetary attraction and a healthy marriage.

Commitment Four:

Turning Our Hearts Toward Our Children

It is common for modern fathers to have their hearts drawn to the pursuit of wealth, personal pleasures, and pastimes. As St. Joseph's Covenant Keepers, we will turn our hearts toward our children. This turning of heart, mind, and life priorities will be especially reflected in the time we devote to our children. We realize that for our children love is a four letter word spelled "t-i-m-e." Since time is money in the modern world, we need to value our children more than money and make them a higher priority.

6

Turning Our Hearts Toward Our Children

"And he will turn the hearts of fathers to their children and the hearts of children to their fathers, lest I come and smite the land with a curse."

—Malachi 4:6

"...you who are ready at the appointed time, it is written, to calm the wrath of God before it breaks out in fury, to turn the heart of the father to the son, and to restore the tribes of Jacob."

—Sirach 48:10

My four-year-old son, John, and I had just finished stacking the seventh bag of composted manure for our backyard planting projects when John straightened his back and exclaimed, "I'm a *real* son." John's declaration came as an early Father's Day present, but it completely caught me off guard. He had never said anything like this before. What had happened to create such feelings in my son?

John and I had worked hard for two hours. Together we dug a hole to plant an orange tree for Matthew's first birthday. We measured, cut, and nailed landscape timbers for a new backyard hedge. Then we cemented a new p.v.c. coupling for a hose faucet. At each step I let John actively participate so he could learn a few work skills. Our final task was unloading seven forty-pound bags of composted cow manure from our van. John knew that this was a "man-sized" task and jumped right in to help.

My son received more esteem building in two hours of sweaty work with me than he could ever get from singing a thousand rounds of "I Am Special" in a classroom. From the dawn of human history until the Industrial Revolution, it was common for fathers and their children, especially sons, to work together. Although the modern era has brought us unparalleled material wealth, it has simultaneously impoverished the bond between a father and his children that is strengthened by laboring together.

Like many fathers, I am constantly tempted to be too busy in my work away from home. Although we had lived in our new home for almost a year, my work schedule prevented me from doing many backyard projects. I was preoccupied with keeping the Family Life Center growing and financially solvent while trying to pay for four different surgeries incurred by family members over the previous year. These may be great reasons to work hard at my job, but they are not good enough reasons to be too busy to work up a sweat with my son.

The really important things in life are the things that have lasting impact. As a father, the time I spend working with my children in the backyard is a way I can impact the world twenty, thirty, or even fifty years from now through my children and, later, my grandchildren. "The father may die, and yet he is not dead, for he has left behind him one like himself" (Sirach 30:4).

Christian men are eager to discover their masculine identity and a masculine spirituality. The discovery of our fatherhood begins and develops within our families. We don't have to travel halfway across the country to find it. We can find our fatherhood in our own backyard. As a double blessing, we may help our sons and daughters discover their identity as well.

How Children Spell "Love"

For children love is a four letter word spelled "t-i-m-e." Children really don't need too many things. However, they do need to have large amounts of time with their father. Family "experts" suggesting that children can get by with only a limited amount of "quality time" are prescribing a formula for parental failure. Children want large quantities of quality time with their fathers.

Years ago as a youth pastor I visited Sunday School classes on Father's Day and asked children to fill in the blank to the following question: "I love my dad because _____." One little boy's reply was unforgettable: "I love my dad because he takes me to the dump on Saturday morning." What was this little guy trying to say about his dad? He didn't mean the dump was his favorite place, but that he and his father had a regular time to be together. Children value the simple times they share with their fathers every week more than expensive, annual trips to a theme park.

I plan my list of Saturday morning errands like a military campaign. First, hit the post office to mail the packages, next charge to the hardware store to get the needed parts for our fix-it jobs, then blitz the auto-parts store, and finally race back home: mission accomplished. Unfortunately, this Saturday morning assault is slowed to a snail's pace if I take the kids along, especially since I have younger children that need to be buckled into car seats. Before I leave I have to spend twenty minutes looking for their shoes and socks. At each stop it's unbuckle and buckle, unbuckle and buckle, interspersed with frequent trips to the bathroom. I must admit that I am often tempted to leave my children at home while doing my errands. Tempted, that is, until I remember that little boy who said, "I love my dad because...."

Peers Replacing Parents

Parents today are living in the most anti-family culture in human history. A dramatic change in family life took place in the twenty years between 1960 and 1980. Since the dawn of recorded history, parents have been the primary influence in shaping an adolescent's behavior and beliefs. Between the 1960s and the 1980s, the peer group replaced parents as the dominant influence in shaping behavior and beliefs.[1] Never before, even in pagan cultures, have parents fallen from the first position.

It is easy to pinpoint the primary reason for this collapse of parental influence. Parents in the 1980s spent 40 percent less time with their children than parents did in the early 1960s.[2] The loss of parents' influence corresponds directly to the loss of parents' time with their children. During the 1990s, parental influence fell even further as the media dramatically increased its impact for shaping morals, values and behavior of young people.[3] The peer group and the media have become the dominant influences in a young person's life. By the time a typical child enters *first grade* he will have spent more hours watching television than he will spend talking to his father in a *lifetime*.[4]

The Secret to Overcoming Negative Peer Pressure

There is one secret to preventing drug abuse, overcoming negative peer pressure, disciplining your children effectively, and raising teens to keep their faith throughout adolescence. That secret is spending large amounts of time with your children. The most important ingredient to parental success is investing time in the lives of your children.

Spending large quantities of time with our children is essential if we want them to adopt our values instead of those of their peergroup. By doing just what other fathers are doing today you can expect your children to adopt the values of their peer group and eventually lose their faith. Although it doesn't get mentioned as often as it should, dads need to remember that such a loss of faith has eternal consequences. As parents, our primary obligation is to make sure our children know, love, and serve God in this life so that they can spend eternity with him in the next.

"When Is Daddy Coming Home?"

Absentee fathers are rapidly becoming the norm.[5] Millions of fathers have left their families through divorce, separation, and abandonment.

However, there is another, more subtle form of paternal abandonment. Many fathers are being consumed by the time devoted to their careers, jobs, and the pursuit of wealth. Every father is called to be a good provider. Therefore, he is expected to devote a substantial amount of every week to provide for the family. For some men, this godly work of "making a living" has been distorted into the goal of "making a (financial) killing." For others, just keeping pace on the financial treadmill takes all their energy. As a result, families are dying.

Restoring Our Priorities

Prioritizing time is critical. Time cannot be recovered. Once it is gone, it is gone forever. Most fathers are sensing a need to adjust their priorities in order to give greater time to their children.

The Old Testament prophet Malachi described the familial, social, and religious deterioration taking place in his day. In chapter four he announces a "great and terrible" day of judgment coming upon the land. In his mercy, God offers a family-based blueprint for restoring the crumbling culture and averting his wrath. "And he will turn the hearts of the fathers to their children and the hearts of children to their fathers, lest I come and smite the land with a curse" (Malachi 4:6). As fathers turn their hearts to their children, children return to the faith and values of their fathers. Spiritual restoration begins when fathers turn their hearts, minds, and life priorities toward their children.

Before we can restore our love for our families, we need to restore our love for God. It is difficult, if not impossible, for us to value our wives and children enough to make significant lifestyle changes until we rediscover the value of God.

We need a radical turning. The Bible calls such a radical turning, "repentance." How are we going to escape the clutches of materialism, provide a good living for our families, and turn our priorities as covenant keepers to our wives and children?

The first step is for fathers to return to God the Father. As we regain value for God we simultaneously regain the ability to see that our wives and children are infinitely more valuable than the pursuit of wealth and pleasure. Adjusting our appointment books becomes easy after we recapture a true sense of value that comes from loving God.

The Paradox of Finding the Time for Fathering

There is a striking paradox in the way we recapture a love for God along with finding the time for fathering.

Recently I received an advertisement for an upgraded computer organizer promising to simplify my life by providing a hundred ways to get more things done faster. The ad even had a picture of a highway billboard that said that I could be home by now if I was using this program.

I really don't think faster computers or upgraded software programs are capable of getting us home sooner. Even though our society travels in the technological fast-lane, we often seem unable to make time breakthroughs in the one area where it really matters: the family.

In past generations, a father's chief challenge was providing enough money. Most contemporary fathers continue to find the task of bread-winning formidable. Yet a greater challenge than finding enough daily bread can be finding enough daily time. How do we find adequate time for our families?

Managing time in a godly fashion is similar to managing money. We either make them our servants, or we become their slaves. The primary way to escape bondage to both time and money is to give the first portion to God in recognition of his Lordship over both. Those men who serve God with their time and money become free men.

It is a challenge to our faith to learn how to "tithe our time," that is, to give God the first part of our time each week in the same way we give him the first part of our financial increase. Our society says, "time is money." For families, time is more valuable than money. Time is essential for a strong family life.

The Ancient Secret of Time Management

Anyone interested in finding family time needs to rediscover God's ancient principle of time management found in one of the ten commandments. It is the only one of the ten commandments that God says to "remember." Amazingly, this is the very commandment we are prone to forget.

> *"Remember the sabbath day, to keep it holy. Six days you shall labor, and do all your work; but the seventh day is a sabbath to the LORD your God; in it you shall not do any work, you, or your son, or your daughter, your manservant, or your maidservant, or your cattle, or the sojourner who is within your gates..."* (Exodus 20:8-10).

By "giving up" our valuable work-time to God at the beginning of every week we gain a sense of proper priorities, eternal values, and life's ultimate purpose. By ordering our week according to the third commandment we gain God's perspective on time. We join in God's eternal rest, refreshing our careworn hearts and wearied bodies. On the other hand, by never getting off the workday treadmill, we create misplaced priorities, neglected families, premature health problems, and mid-life crises.

At the end of our lives, we will never regret spending too little time at the office. But we will always regret spending too little time with our families. How can we learn wisdom about prioritizing our time before our time is spent?

Giving Time to God, Finding Time for Family

The secret to good time management is to obey the third commandment. Those who make time for God on Sunday and take a day off from daily work will find the proper amount of time for their families all week long.

Samuel Dresner, Jewish theologian and author of *Can Families Survive in Pagan America?,* points out the strong connection between the third and fourth commandments. He writes:

> As truly as the Sabbath is a day for the renewal of the individual, it is equally and uniquely a day for the family. No matter how exhausting and frantic the workaday week has been—often pulling family members into different and distant directions ... the arrival of the Sabbath ... sweeps all before it, closing the mind to work-day worries, collecting the scattered family.... It is no accident that in the Ten Commandments the commandment to 'honor thy father and thy mother' follows the Sabbath commandment.[6]

In the New Testament St. Paul exhorts us to carefully consider our time and family priorities. "Look carefully then how you walk, not as unwise men but as wise, making the most of the time, because the days are evil. Therefore do not be foolish, but understand what the will of the LORD is" (Ephesians 5:15-17). After encouraging the wise use of time, St. Paul goes on to discuss marriage and family relationships in Ephesians 5 and 6.

The new catechism also connects family life with observance of the third commandment: "Christians will also sanctify Sunday by devoting time and care to their families and relatives, often difficult to do on other days of the week."[7]

Here are seven practical ways to observe the third commandment and to make time for your family:

1. Attend church every week with your family.

St. Paul in Ephesians 5:14 says, "Awake, O sleeper, and arise from the dead, and Christ shall give you light." Get out of bed on Sunday morning and take your whole family to Mass! Don't let your wife take your children to church alone. Also, never drop your children off while you skip Mass and go home to read the Sunday paper. Lead by example and insist that your whole family worship together every Sunday.

2. Take a day off from your work.

Men who do not take one day off a week become slaves to their work, lose their sense of priorities, and inevitably spend inadequate time with their families. Get off the treadmill one day a week and refresh yourself in God's eternal rest. It is the only way to keep your time and priorities in balance. Fathers cannot afford to neglect the third commandment.

3. Arrange your shopping and business affairs so that others can take a day off from work also.

A few years ago my wife, Karen, had the opportunity to sponsor a single mother with two young children who was entering the Church. Karen and I were upset when her employer required her to work Sundays in the supermarket deli. If more Christians did their shopping on Saturday instead of Sunday, then people like this single mother might enjoy Sundays at church and at home with their children. In Exodus 20, God told the Israelites not even to make their cattle work on the Sabbath. Shouldn't we at least do the same for our neighbor, particularly those in service-oriented jobs? The new catechism says, "Every Christian should avoid making unnecessary demands on others that would hinder them from observing the Lord's Day."[8]

4. Make your entire Sunday a family day.

After attending Mass, try to spend the rest of the day together. Sunday is not the best time for sporting activities apart from the family. Spend the day together in recreational activities.

5. Have a family meal at least once a day. (The evening meal is best.)

A recent survey of teens showed that high school students who seldom (or never) eat dinner together with their families are almost four times as likely to engage in premarital intercourse and half as likely to spend time studying than those teens who regularly eat dinner with their families.[9] The National Center on Addiction and Substance Abuse at Columbia University reports that teens who regularly eat dinner with their family and attend church with their parents are less likely to use drugs.[10]

Turn off the television during your family meal and enjoy conversation with your wife and children. There is no such thing as having a family meal while the television is on. The tube turns a family meal into a TV dinner.

6. Ask God to place *his* priorities in your heart.

The years of our life are threescore and ten, or even by reason of strength fourscore; yet their span is but toil and trouble; they are soon gone, and we fly away.... So teach us to number our days that we may get a heart of wisdom (Psalm 90:10, 12).

7. Write down your primary goal in life on a piece of paper.

Write down the most important thing you want to accomplish in life. May I suggest the goal of having your family continue together for eternity in heaven? The Sabbath in the Old Testament and Sunday in the New Testament are foretastes of the eternal rest we will enjoy with Christ after the second advent. The family who worships, prays, and plays together on Sunday stays together not just for a lifetime, but forever. The father who spends time with God and his family on Sunday is helping his family prepare for heaven. Make your time count for eternity by offering Christ the first day of your week. God will return to you a life lived wisely along with everlasting life to enjoy with your family.

Fathers, Come Home!

Fathers, be covenant keepers by returning to God and returning to your children! Love God, then love your children by sacrificing your time to be with them. Follow the example of St. Joseph who is always depicted with his son Jesus. There are only a few years in which to make an eternal difference in the lives of your children. Nothing else you touch approximates their worth. Invest your time wisely.

Fathers, come home! The future of the world and the Church depends on your presence in and with your family. There is no person, or thing, that can substitute for you. Your children need you. Fathers who generously spend time with their children in this life have a much greater likelihood of enjoying their eternal presence in heaven.

Commitment Five:

Educating Our Children in the Discipline and Instruction of the Lord

Parents are the first and primary educators of their children. Fathers are particularly singled out in Scripture for the religious education and training of their children (Genesis 18:19, Psalm 78, Ephesians 6:4). This high privilege and duty of fathers teaching the faith to their children will result in a faith that will persevere through adolescent questionings, peer pressure, and university life.

7

Educating Our Children in the Discipline and Instruction of the Lord

"Fathers, do not provoke your children to anger but bring them up in the discipline and instruction of the LORD."
—Ephesians 6:4

"...this is my covenant with them, says the LORD: my spirit which is upon you, and my words which I have put in your mouth, shall not depart out of your mouth, or out of the mouth of your children, or out of the mouth of your children's children, says the LORD, from this time forth and for evermore."
—Isaiah 59:21

I was utterly exhausted as I hiked up the moonlit hill with my arms full of chocolate. Pausing to rest outside our cabin, I offered a short prayer for the eight hungry boys waiting inside. I asked God for strength and for a blessing on the boys, but I never imagined the miracle I would witness that night.

As a college student, I had volunteered to be the chief counselor for a week-long camp high in the California Sierras. My responsibility was to coordinate fifteen hours of non-stop activities every day for a hundred children. Along with their regular duties, all the other counselors had to supervise a cabin of eight to ten children. Since I had the formidable task of keeping the whole camp occupied during waking hours, I was supposed to have a special cabin with no campers so that I could get a decent night's sleep.

We had put all the boys with severe behavioral and psychological problems into one cabin. Managing these troubled boys would be one of the toughest challenges of the camp. Therefore, one counselor's only job was supervising this special cabin. Two days before camp began, this counselor got sick. Guess who got his cabin?

Although we had a rocky start, by midweek the boys and I were developing a sense of camaraderie. I wanted to change this gang of uncooperative juveniles into a willing and energetic team, so I made them a deal. If they kept our cabin in top shape for the week, I promised them all the chocolate they could eat on the last night of the camp. It worked. Each morning all the boys were up early working to make sure the cabin passed inspection with flying colors.

One of my camp activities was building a rope bridge across a ravine. The boys from my cabin gradually quit their trouble-making and joined the rest of the camp in tackling this challenge. We worked overtime to finish the bridge by the last day of camp. Boys who wouldn't lift a finger earlier in the week were now dripping with sweat to help finish the job. We were filled with a sense of accomplishment. We had made something with our owns hands that we had only seen before in movies.

Now I was standing outside the cabin under the stars holding boxes of chocolate. I had never felt so drained of energy. However, I had one important job left. Not only had I built a rope bridge with these boys, but I had consciously spent the week building a relational bridge with them as well. My relationship with these difficult boys was at a high point and I knew that I had a once in a lifetime opportunity to share Christ with them. "Please," I implored God, "just give me enough strength to finish the job."

I stepped into the cabin and told the boys that I had their reward. Whooping with excitement, they leaped from their bunks. I lit a couple of candles and asked them to sit in a circle on the floor. I wanted to give them a brief scriptural survey of God's saving plan in history before distributing the candy. I wasn't halfway through when one of the boys started crying and gently shaking. I recognized that the Holy Spirit had descended upon him in a special way.

Overwhelmed with the presence of God, the boy repeated softly, "God really loves me! God really loves me!" God's Spirit spread to the other boys. While the rest of the camp slept, we received an outpouring of God's grace. Our little cabin, which six days earlier had been filled with crude speech and profanity, was now lost in a timeless experience of intimate prayer and praise. It was awe-inspiring to see such a manifestation of divine power transforming the hearts of these formerly troubled boys.

I have no idea when our prayer time ended. I sent the boys to bed and went outside to thank God for sending us a little Pentecost. Then I realized that we had completely forgotten about the chocolate. I returned to the cabin and roused the boys for a few minutes of gorging on the sweet candy.

Within twenty-four hours one father told me that that week had transformed his son. This father took one look at his son climbing into the station wagon and realized that he was seeing a new person.

That week also changed me. Sharing our faith with others always creates a two-way transformation. As a single man, I had seen what spending just a week in the mountains with some boys could do. Many times since, I have thought, "If I could have such an impact over the course of a week, what could a father do over the course of two decades?"

Strength of Faith Conveyed = Strength of Relationship Made

Even before the camp, I knew that building relational bridges was the key to conveying our faith to children. Shortly after my adult conversion to Christ, I found myself in charge of one the largest and fastest-growing Christian youth ministries in Southern California. I had almost no experience. I had only the desire of permanently influencing the children in my care. I wanted to discover the secret for creating a lifelong impression, so I conducted an informal survey among my classmates at a Christian college. I asked them which Sunday school teacher had had the most profound effect on their lives. Their answers were always similar: "Mrs. Johnson, who always took us to the park," or "Mr. Foster, who took us fishing," or "Miss Garcia, who took us to the zoo."

They never identified their most influential teacher as the one who was best at teaching theology in the classroom. Their best teacher was always the one who took time to be with his students outside the classroom. I realized that the strength of the faith conveyed was directly proportionate to the strength of the relationship between the teacher and the student. With this little bit of insight on how to pass on the faith, I began to build a successful youth ministry.

My discovery that a relational bridge is the key to passing on the faith is nothing new. This successful method of conveying the faith is several thousand years old.

Imparting the Faith in the Course of Everyday Life

After the Exodus, Moses commanded the Israelite parents to share their faith with their children while they shared their everyday life. The faith transmitted in this way would stick even in the pagan environment the Israelites were about to enter.

> *"And these words which I command you this day shall be upon your heart; and you shall teach them diligently to your children, and shall talk of them when you sit in your house, and when you walk by the way, and when you lie down, and when you rise"* (Deuteronomy 6:6-7).

Fathers Educating Their Children in the Faith

In the Old Testament, Abraham is the model father for teaching the faith to his children. About four thousand years ago, God revealed to Abraham his plan of blessing the world through Abraham's family. How could God be sure that Abraham would pass the faith down to his descendants? God knew that Abraham would not subcontract the job of teaching his children. He knew that Abraham would personally educate his children in the faith.

The faith is much more than abstract religious ideas conveyed in a classroom. True religious faith grips the heart and mind and animates every aspect of life. For the faith to persist in challenging times, children need instruction in both word and deed from someone who cares about them. Classroom religious instruction, while certainly valuable, often produces *ideas* about God. Family religious instruction produces a *faith* that becomes a permanent way of life.

Genesis 18:17-19 describes God's covenant promise to bless Abraham's descendants because this covenant father would personally instruct his children in "the way of the LORD."

> *"...Abraham shall become a great and mighty nation, and all the nations of the earth shall bless themselves by him ... for I have chosen him, that he may charge his children and his household after him to keep the way of the LORD by doing righteousness and justice; so that the LORD may bring to Abraham what he has promised him"* (Genesis 18:17-19).

What Works When All Else Fails?

Someone might object saying: "Abraham's difficulties were nothing compared to our contemporary challenges. Look at our corrupt society! Are you trying to convince me that a four-thousand-year-old catechizing strategy will still work today?"

Yes, I am not only claiming that fathers can effectively catechize their children in today's deteriorating culture, but I maintain that this is the *only* strategy that will work in a wicked civilization. Take a close look at the context of Genesis 18:17-19. The verses before and after this passage soberly relate God's plan to judge and destroy the cities of Sodom and Gomorrah. By personally instructing their children, fathers can successfully impart the faith even in the midst of degeneracy. Just because our culture is self-destructing doesn't mean that our family and our faith must perish along with it.

Transmitting the Faith for Generations

Every Christian father can follow Abraham's example of personally instructing his children. Psalm 78 highlights the powerful multi-generational effects of fathers teaching their children the faith.

> *We will ... tell to the coming generation the glorious deeds of the LORD, and his might, and the wonders which he has wrought. He established a testimony in Jacob, and appointed a law in Israel, which he commanded our fathers to teach to their children; that the next generation might know them, the children yet unborn, and arise and tell them to their children, so that they should set their hope in God, and not forget the works of God, but keep his*

commandments; and that they should not be like their fathers, a stubborn and rebellious generation, a generation whose heart was not steadfast, whose spirit was not faithful to God (Psalm 78:4-8).

Psalm 78 emphasizes that when a father teaches the faith to his children, he is also passing on the faith to his grandchildren and great-grandchildren who are not yet born. When he personally instructs his children, a father not only conveys the content of the faith, but also models the world's best teaching method. The strong bond he shares with his children makes his instruction effective. A son will grow up to follow the example of his father and take the time to teach the faith to his children as well.[1] This is God's timeless plan for passing on the faith within a family for generations.

Keeping Your Teens Catholic

In the United States, the Catholic faith is not being successfully handed on to the younger generation. Millions of Catholic parents mourn the loss of faith in their children. Even with years of Catholic education, children are abandoning their faith in alarming numbers. For example, consider the number of young Catholics who hold erroneous beliefs about the Blessed Eucharist, the center of the Catholic faith. A *New York Times* and CBS News poll of Catholics who attend Mass regularly found that only 17 percent of people between the ages of eighteen and twenty-nine believe in the Real Presence. Seventy percent of young Catholics believe that the Eucharist is merely symbolic.[2]

In the midst of such an unprecedented loss of faith among young Catholics, only one strategy is capable of passing on the faith in a way that sticks: fathers catechizing their children. This is what works in a Teflon culture that resists any attempt to teach morality and truth. Psalm 78:7-8 promises that if fathers will teach the faith to their children, the faith will not be forgotten or cast aside in rebellion. It will stay with them for life. "Train up a child in the way he should go, and when he is old he will not depart from it" (Proverbs 22:6).

The Holy Father emphasizes the importance of parents catechizing their children in the home:

Family catechesis therefore precedes, accompanies and enriches all other forms of catechesis. Furthermore, **in places where widespread unbelief or invasive secularism makes real religious growth practically impossible, the Church of the home remains the one place where children and young people can receive an authentic catechesis**. Thus there cannot be too great an effort on the part of Christian parents to prepare for this ministry of being their own children's catechists and to carry it out with tireless zeal. Encouragement must also be given to the individuals or institutions that, through person-to-person contacts, through meetings, and through all kinds of pedagogical means, help parents to perform their task: the service they are doing to catechesis is beyond price.[3]

Dads, "The Buck Stops Here"

Some fathers, convinced of passing on the faith through the family, might be saying to themselves, "I need to get my wife doing this right away." Dads, this responsibility rests on *your* shoulders. In a passage of scripture that discusses both spouses, St. Paul singles out fathers for the chief responsibility in passing on the faith. "Fathers, do not provoke your children to anger, but bring them up in the discipline and instruction of the LORD" (Ephesians 6:4). Obviously your wife should help teach the faith to your children, but to paraphrase President Truman, the buck stops with you! As a father, God has given you a unique spiritual authority in your relationship with your children. You are their primary spiritual teacher. Parish and school religious education are secondary programs to reinforce, not replace, what you do in the home.

How well are fathers fulfilling their duty to teach the faith? A survey of Christian families asked parents with children under eighteen years old, "Which parent spends more time discussing religion?" Forty-eight percent indicated that mothers spent more time while only 11 percent said fathers did.[4] Fathers have some catching up to do.

The Holy Father, John Paul II, is calling fathers to be actively involved in their families, especially in education:

Above all where social and cultural conditions so easily encourage a father to be less concerned with his family or at any rate less involved in the work of education, efforts must be made to restore socially the conviction that **the place and task of the father in and for the family is of unique and irreplaceable importance."**[5]

How to Overcome the Fear of Teaching

While the responsibility of teaching your kids may seem formidable, it is actually nothing to fear.

As a Protestant minister, I learned a lesson about the paralyzing effects of fear. We had formed a new congregation with a specific focus on families. We wanted to build our congregation by ministering to families with young children. When it came time to recruit Sunday school teachers I was bewildered and discouraged that no one volunteered to teach, even after repeated pleas for teachers. Hadn't we agreed to focus on young families? I became upset thinking I was pastoring a flock that lacked commitment. During one service I just blurted out my frustration: "Why doesn't anyone want to teach Sunday school in this congregation?" The bravest man in the congregation hesitantly raised his hand and said, "We are scared to teach because we don't know how."

This man's frank admission helped me see the obvious: we dread and avoid the things we don't know how to do. I ordered an early grade curriculum and asked my wife, Karen, to teach an initial class. Then I asked for volunteers to simply watch Karen teach. After watching her teach for a few weeks, they willingly began to help. Before long they felt confident and comfortable in assuming the responsibility of teaching their own classes. We asked for more volunteers to observe these new classes and multiplied our recruiting opportunities. After discovering this method of easing fears through observation and gradual participation, we never had another problem recruiting teachers.

Most men would never dream of catechizing their children. It's not that they don't want to, or that they don't love their children enough. They simply don't know how. I'll never forget the burly New York City policeman who came up to me with tears streaming down his face, saying, "My dad never taught me, so I don't know how to teach my kids their faith. But I want to learn how." It takes a lot of courage for a man to admit that he doesn't know his faith well enough to teach it.

It is safe to say that the majority of men born after World War II don't know their faith well enough to instruct their children. What should these men do? They should get some low-stress opportunities to observe other men teaching their children. They should also find some non-threatening opportunities for training in catechesis. There is an effective and easy way to do this.

A Primary Objective for Men's Small Groups

Interest in men's ministry is sweeping the country. Many Catholic men want to start small groups. We get numerous calls from men asking, "What should we do with our men's ministry?"

First, we recommend setting long-term goals. One good way to establish a long-term goal is to simply ask, "What can our men's group do this year that will bear fruit in the lives of our children, grandchildren, and great-grandchildren?" For men's small groups, this is the sixty-four thousand dollar question.

One small group activity that stands above all the rest in producing lasting fruit is training fathers to teach the faith to their children. Men's small groups are the perfect place to prepare fathers to catechize their children. Pope John Paul II emphasizes that the value of helping parents instruct their children is "beyond price."[6]

There are some practical ways a small group can help fathers assume the role of family catechist. Begin by discussing the many scriptures that specifically exhort fathers to hand on the faith to their children. Acknowledge your obligation to personally instruct your children in the faith. Then, give fathers the practical tools to accomplish this task.[7] Experienced catechists, particularly the older men in your group, can show the younger men how to teach their children. God calls grandfathers along with fathers to make the faith "known to [their] children and [their] children's children" (Deuteronomy 4:9-10; also see Isaiah 59:21).

Fathers teaching the faith to their children is what works even when a culture has collapsed. Family catechesis is the secret to preserving our children's faith. Fathers need to be equipped, encouraged, and held mutually accountable to fulfill their obligation to educate their children in the faith. Men's small groups can provide priceless assistance to fathers wanting to fulfill the fifth commitment of St. Joseph's Covenant Keepers. Groups that equip and encourage men to catechize their children can transform the world for generations to come.

You Gotta Follow Through

This spring I was teaching my son, John, how to hit a baseball. I showed him that if he doesn't follow through with his swing, he'll never hit a home run. Likewise, if you don't follow through with your children's religious education, they may not get to their heavenly home base. It doesn't do any good to sacrifice eighteen years personally catechizing your children, nurturing their faith, and protecting them from temptations if they jettison their faith after a few years of college, for which you have paid tens of thousands of dollars! That's like knocking a baseball out of the ballpark, and forgetting to tag home plate.

No longer can Catholic parents send their children to the nearest Catholic college, trusting that it will preserve their faith. In many Catholic colleges, skeptical scripture scholars and dissenting theologians teach that the Bible is unreliable, that the Gospel miracles are second-century "inventions," and that Catholics can conscientiously ignore the Church's unpopular moral teachings. Sending your children to a nominally Catholic college may be the quickest way to destroy their faith.[8]

If you look at a college directory, you will find dozens of schools calling themselves Catholic, but only a few are worthy of the name. In choosing a Catholic college, you have an obligation to find an institution that teaches the Catholic faith without distortion, lives the Catholic faith without compromise, and nourishes the Catholic faith without apology.

As fathers educating our children for eternity, we must diligently search out those Catholic institutions that still combine orthodoxy and academic excellence.[9] Choosing a college is one of the most important decisions your family can make. Your child's college experience will often determine his future faith, occupation, marriage partner, and outlook on life.

A father's catechetical responsibilities don't end with high school. Fathers, as the primary educators of your children, you need to follow through and preserve your children's faith throughout their college years.

Commitment Six:

Protecting Our Families

As fathers, we will protect our families from physical, spiritual, and moral harm. We will take personal responsibility, and an active role to preserve our children's chastity. We will protect them from everything that disturbs or destroys the fragile nature of our children's sexual latency, innocence, and purity.

8

Protecting Our Families

> "...an angel of the LORD appeared to Joseph in a dream and said, 'Rise, take the child and his mother, and flee to Egypt, and remain there till I tell you; for Herod is about to search for the child, to destroy him.' And he rose and took the child and his mother by night, and departed to Egypt.... Then Herod ... sent and killed all the male children in Bethlehem who were two years old or under...."
>
> —Matthew 2:13-14, 16

Herod's troops were about to launch a search-and-destroy mission for the Messiah. The very life of Jesus was at stake. Through a dream, God sent a warning to St. Joseph, the head of the Holy Family, to flee to Egypt. God's plan for the salvation of the world hinged upon the decisive and instant obedience of this Hebrew carpenter. St. Joseph rose to the occasion and put the protection of the child Jesus before his career, his home, his friends, and his temporal well-being. Fathers following in the footsteps of St. Joseph realize that protecting their family is as important as providing for their family. Just as St. Joseph was "Guardian of the Redeemer"[1] so we need to be guardians of our families.

Something more dangerous than Herod's troops threatens our children today. Herod's soldiers could only send the Holy Innocents to their graves. Contemporary fathers need to protect their children against forces that can both corrupt their souls and send them to hell. The stakes are high when our children's eternal destinies hang in the balance. For some fathers, this chapter may be a midnight wake-up call.

Protecting Your Children's Innocence

My wife, Karen, and I will never forget the shock we experienced on Sunday, October 6, 1990. As recent converts we were excited about our newly discovered Catholic faith. We enrolled our daughters in religious education classes and were eager to see how the Church would help us teach them the faith.

On the Sunday evening after their first class we made a big bowl of popcorn and sat down to review the religious education materials our daughters brought home. It is difficult to express the utter dismay and alarm we felt as we examined our fourth grader's *The New Creation Series* sex education book, which explicitly described a boy's erection.[2]

With my pro-life background, it was easy to see that this book was a thinly veiled Planned Parenthood type of curriculum. I removed my girls from the classes immediately. I could not entrust my children to teachers and programs that were playing into the heart of the pro-abortion strategy for passing on the sexual revolution to the next generation.

This explicit sex-ed curriculum was accompanied by a letter explaining that such programs were necessary because the media was exposing children to sexuality. Their reasoning was that since children have already been overexposed to sex by the media we should expose them to classroom sex-ed. A much wiser statement comes from The Pontifical Council for the Family's document, *The Truth and Meaning of Human Sexuality: Guidelines for Education within the Family,* which says "explicit and premature sex education can never be justified in the name of a prevailing secularized culture."[3]

Fortunately, the parish soon got rid of *The New Creation Series.* Unfortunately, they replaced it with one that was even worse: *Valuing Your Sexuality*, a program adapted for the Catholic Church by Nancy Hennessy Cooney. Ms. Cooney's guidelines asked parents to sit in a circle and discuss topics like adolescent sex-play with other children and relating to friends who have made different "lifestyle" choices.

The Connection Between Abortion and Sex-Ed

I discovered that Ms. Cooney was one of the persons who proudly signed the "solidarity ad" in the *New York Times,* on March 2, 1986, supporting abortion.[4] If Ms. Cooney believes that a morally valid "choice" can sometimes include killing innocent babies, then how can she be trusted to help children make decisions about masturbation, homosexuality, and sexual relations outside of marriage?

Informed pro-lifers know that there is a long-standing connection between abortion and sex education. Alan Guttmacher was a former president of Planned Parenthood, the world's largest provider of abortion. After the 1973 *Roe v. Wade* decision, a reporter asked him how he planned to keep abortion legal and prevent the Supreme Court's decision from being reversed. Guttmacher gave an unforgettable two-word reply: "Sex education."[5]

Alan Guttmacher, like his predecessor Margaret Sanger, knew that abortion is the fruit of the sexual revolution. He realized that the only way to keep abortion legal is to keep the sexual revolution going. Planned Parenthood's scheme for perpetuating the sexual revolution is sex education. Explicit, classroom-style sex education fans the fires of the sexual revolution which in turn drives the demand for abortion.

Madalyn Murray O'Hair, the atheist responsible for getting prayer banned from public schools, was very candid: "The issue of abortion is a red herring. Until it dawns on the combatants that the fight is over sex education, including information on birth control, the battle will continue...."[6]

The Family Room is the Best Classroom

Thankfully, the Vatican recently published *The Truth and Meaning of Human Sexuality: Guidelines for Education within the Family.* This document is a Magna Carta of parental rights in sexual education and an answer to many parents' prayers. As expressed in the title of this document, the Pontifical Council for the Family advocates that education in human sexuality be done "*within* the family." Its central thesis is that sex education belongs in the family room, not the classroom: "the family is, in fact, the best environment to accomplish the obligation of securing a gradual education in the sexual life."[7]

Can sexual morality and chastity ever be legitimately taught in Catholic classrooms? Of course it can, but only in a specific way. For almost two thousand years, the Catholic Church has taught sexual morality in the ordinary course of catechesis on the sixth and ninth commandments. The timeless wisdom of the Church has urged caution, delicacy, and moderation in teaching these two commandments.[8]

How to Teach the Mystery of Marital Love

There is an inescapable reason why classroom sex education will result in moral failure. The act of spousal love within marriage is the most intimate and sacred of human relationships. Spousal love is inherently private. Classroom sex education makes public something that is by nature private and intimate. To treat the sacred as though it was common is to profane it. Classroom sex education profanes the sacredness of married love. A subject needs to be taught in a manner consistent with its nature. Since spousal love is inherently private and intimate it must be taught that way. Dragging this sacred mystery into public view cheapens the gift of marital sexuality. The new *Catechism of the Catholic Church* says:

> Purity requires modesty, an integral part of temperance. Modesty protects the intimate center of the person. It means refusing to unveil what should remain hidden.... Modesty protects the mystery of persons and their love. It keeps silence or reserve where there is risk of unhealthy curiosity. It is discreet.[9]

Even well-intentioned chastity programs can backfire by overfocusing on the subject. For instance, suicide prevention programs often result in higher suicide rates among teens who have gone through them. This is true of some drug-prevention courses as well. Why? These programs focus too much on subjects that should be treated with brevity and delicacy.

Preserving the "Years of Innocence"

Children don't need to be bombarded with sexual information. God has built within childhood a period of sexual latency, a time when children naturally have little interest in sex. "[F]rom about five years of age until puberty ... a child is in the stage described in John Paul II's words as 'the years of innocence....' " This period of tranquillity and serenity must never be disturbed by unnecessary information about sex. During those years ... it is normal for the child's interests to turn to other aspects of life."[10]

Pope Pius XI's encyclical *On the Christian Education of Youth* contains the most authoritative Church teaching on preserving innocence when educating youth in sexuality:

> Far too common is the error of those who with dangerous assurance and under an ugly term propagate a so-called sex-education, falsely imagining they can forearm youths against the dangers of sensuality by means purely natural, such as **a foolhardy initiation and precautionary instruction for all indiscriminately, even in public; and, worse still, by exposing them at an early age** to the occasions, in order to accustom them, so it is argued, and as it were to harden them against such dangers. Such persons grievously err in refusing to recognize the inborn weakness of human nature....

> Such is our misery and inclination to sin, that often in the very things considered to be remedies against sin, we find occasions for and inducements to sin itself. Hence **it is of the highest importance that a good father, while discussing with his son a matter so delicate, should be well on his guard and not descend to details**, nor refer to the various ways in which this infernal hydra destroys with its poison so large a portion of the world; **otherwise it may happen that instead of extinguishing the fire, he unwittingly stirs or kindles it in the simple and tender heart of the child**. Speaking generally, during the period of childhood it suffices to employ those remedies which produce the double effect of opening the door to the virtue of purity and closing the door upon vice.[11]

Protect your children from anything that disturbs their sexual latency, especially classroom sex education. Once your child's God-given latency period is violated, it is gone forever. Don't just shift this responsibility to your wife. You have the right and the obligation to remove your children from any kind of education you deem unsuitable.[12]

Protecting Your Teen

Many fathers think that only babies, toddlers, and young children need home supervision. If you are the father of a teen, think again. Sexual immorality among teenagers at home is causing a potential tidal wave of ruined marriages.

Fathers who grew up in the sixties might think that sexual temptation for teens takes place at Lover's Lane or at the drive-in. Look around: Lover's Lane is now a subdivision and the drive-in is now a shopping mall. So now where do most teens break the sixth commandment? In your own *home*, maybe even in your own *bed*! This can come as a shock to many parents.

Home is the place where today's teens get into the most trouble. "Three out of five teens who have sex do so at home when their parents are away, and four out of five students who drink do so at their parents' or friends' houses when the parents are away."[13]

Some Catholic dads might exclaim, "My kid would never do that! We're Catholics!" Unfortunately, one study shows that promiscuity rates among Catholic teens in the home may be even *higher* than among non-Catholics. Researchers investigating 1,228 U.S. parochial students found that "three out of four [sexually active] teenagers reported using someone's home for the location of first sexual experiences. It appears that an empty and unsupervised home provides more opportunity for the adolescent as well as for the younger grade-school latchkey child to engage in sex."[14]

Another study done by Michigan State University and the University of Wisconsin/Madison found that unchaste teenagers are likely to come from homes "where parents do not monitor them [teenagers] closely and hold permissive values regarding teen sexual behavior." This study showed "a very clear association between the level of parental monitoring and sexual experience for both males and females."[15]

Protecting Your Children's (and Grandchildren's) Marriages

Michael McManus, in his book *Marriage Savers*, cites two secular studies showing that people who have engaged in premarital intercourse have a 53 percent to 71 percent higher probability of divorce.[16] In concrete terms, this means a 53 percent to 71 percent increased probability that your grandchildren will grow up without fathers.

It doesn't stop there. Children who come from divorced homes are far more likely to become divorced themselves. According to studies reported by David Blankenhorn in *Fatherless America,* "Daughters of single parents are 92 percent more likely to dissolve their own marriages."[17] The probability of divorce snowballs with every generation that suffers it. Premarital sex does more than increase the probability of divorce for spouses; it dramatically increases the odds that their children and grandchildren will suffer from divorce as well.

These statistics certainly don't prove that if your teen engages in premarital sex that your great-grandchildren will automatically grow up in fatherless families. However, the statistics do warn of a potential avalanche of catastrophes triggered by a lack of adequate supervision. The way you supervise your teen today will have effects for generations to come.

Fathers of teens and younger children should take a close look at the seventh commitment of St. Joseph's Covenant Keepers that reads, in part, "We will seek to provide the maximum opportunity for our wives to nurture our children at home." It is worth sacrificing material comforts and pleasures to provide the opportunity for our wives to be at home for our teens. In situations where it is financially impossible for your wife to be at home, then seek the active help of grandparents, relatives, friends, and neighbors.

Protecting Your Children's Faith

More than two-thirds of Catholic teens quit practicing their faith by the time they leave their teen years. Why? Among the many causes that contribute to this spiritual shipwreck, there is one fatal torpedo sure to sink the faith of teens: sexual immorality. Ironically, this is the one sin that both teens and adults think they can engage in without damaging their faith.

It is no accident that the striking loss of faith among teens has coincided with the sexual revolution. Proverbs 7 warns youth that "many a victim" and "a mighty host" have been led into the paths to hell through sexual immorality. St. Paul warns Timothy to "flee youthful lusts." As a person (and a culture) falls into more degrading degrees of lust and licentiousness the mind becomes progressively darkened to the light of faith (Romans 1:18-32; Ephesians 4:17-19). The loss of chastity frequently leads to the loss of faith.

The inroads of the sexual revolution among teens is staggering. Researchers found that "72 percent of all students by their senior year of high school report having sexual intercourse."[18] The same researchers noted that the Center for Disease Control found the largest jump in sexual activity is among teens under sixteen. The Christian faith of the next generation is being blown out of the water by rampant sexual immorality.

How can we stop teens from acting immorally and losing their faith? Teens need parents to teach them chaste behavior and to warn them about the consequences of promiscuity. Repeatedly, the Scriptures show parents teaching sexual morality.[19] Parents who reject permissive values, teach positive values, and who closely monitor their teens (both male and female) can make a crucial difference in their moral life.

Protecting Yourself So You Can Protect Your Children

Fathers have a natural desire to safeguard their children. However, before fathers can protect their children, they need to protect themselves. If an airplane loses cabin pressure, parents are instructed to place an oxygen mask on themselves *first* and then place one on their child. Otherwise, while attempting to save his child, a well-meaning parent could pass out from lack of oxygen and cause both to become helpless.

Fathers need to include themselves in their protective instincts. Divorce not only rips apart a marriage, it usually tears a father from his children. Close to half of those children with divorced parents have not seen their non-resident parent (usually dad) during the past year.[20] Ten years after a divorce, almost two-thirds of children have not seen their father for a year.[21] Divorce separates fathers from their children. Absent fathers cannot protect their children. Therefore, fathers who are serious about their guardian role will take precautions to guard themselves against any kind of "marriage-buster."

Avoiding the Most Common Marriage-Buster

The most common marriage-buster is adultery. Frequently, those who cheat on their spouses wind up in a divorce court. If you love your children and want to protect them, then remain faithful to your wife by guarding your eyes and watching your actions—very carefully.

Heeding the scriptural warnings against sexual sin will help us remain pure. For example, many men fall into sexual sin because they think no one will see their actions. Sirach reminds us that nothing escapes God's keen sight.

> *A man who breaks his marriage vows says to himself, "Who sees me? Darkness surrounds me, and the walls hide me, and no one sees me. Why should I fear? The Most High will not take notice of my sins." His fear is confined to the eyes of men, and he does not realize that the eyes of the LORD are ten thousand times brighter than the sun; they look upon all the ways of men, and perceive even the hidden places.... This man will be punished in the streets of the city, and where he least suspects it, he will be seized* (Sirach 23:18-19, 21).

Can You Get Away With It?

People who commit adultery always think they can get away with it. They don't think they will suffer any consequences. However, Proverbs promises that no one can escape the results of adultery. This sin will burn you every time.

> *...an adulteress stalks a man's very life. Can a man carry fire in his bosom and his clothes not be burned? Or can one walk upon hot coals and his feet not be scorched? So is he who goes in to his neighbor's wife; none who touches her will go unpunished* (Proverbs 6:26-29).

Adulterers always get burned because, as St. Paul warns, adultery joins a man to "the other woman."

> *Do you not know that your bodies are members of Christ? Shall I therefore take the members of Christ and make them members of a prostitute? Never! Do you not know that he who joins himself to a prostitute becomes one body with her? For, as it is written, "The two shall become one flesh." But he who is united to the LORD becomes one spirit with him. Shun immorality. Every other sin which a man commits is outside the body; but the immoral man sins against his own body* (1 Corinthians 6:15-18).

God designed the sexual embrace to cause a profound union of persons. There is no such thing as "casual sex." Sexual union with a woman outside of your marriage creates an adultery-bond that mimics and wars against your marriage-bond. These two antagonistic bonds produce cataclysmic friction within your own heart and within your marriage. Your wife—who, like God, is jealous of your love—will notice if someone else has a claim on your heart. These so-called "casual affairs" violate the inner sanctity of your marriage. St. Paul says that adultery is a very real, very intimate attack against God and your spouse. You cannot escape the effects of this sin.

Avoiding the Occasions of Sin

How does a husband and father avoid sexual sin in a sex-saturated society? A wise father doesn't take his young, attractive secretary out to a nightclub, have a few drinks, and then start praying "lead us not into temptation."

A wise man avoids sexual sin by avoiding those occasions that lead to sin. Fathers need to treat sexual temptation the way soldiers treat land mines: by staying as far away as possible. Wise men acknowledge their vulnerability to sexual temptation and diligently avoid those things that lead to, or stir up, sexual sin. Fools delude themselves into thinking they can handle any temptation. "Keep your way far from her [a loose woman], and do not go near the door of her house" (Proverbs 5:8).

Making a Covenant With Your Eyes

It is no mystery how sexual temptations start. For men, sexual temptation comes through our eyes. In his Sermon on the Mount, Jesus delivered an unforgettable warning about guarding our sight.

> *"You have heard that it was said, 'You shall not commit adultery.' But I say to you that every one who looks at a woman lustfully has already committed adultery with her in his heart. If your right eye causes you to sin, pluck it out and throw it away; it is better that you lose one of your members than that your whole body be thrown into hell"* (Matthew 5:27-29).

Jesus is speaking in hyperbole. He doesn't intend for us to literally pluck out our eyes, but Jesus does mean that we should take radical measures to cut off any source of temptation. We must get rid of everything in our lives that is sexually suggestive or explicit. Ditch the dirty magazines. Incinerate the indecent videos. Cancel the carnal cable channels. The more we allow adulterous scenes to come into our minds, the more likely we will have adulterous thoughts and inclinations.

We Christian fathers need to follow the example of godly Job and guard our eyes from impurity: "I have made a covenant with my eyes; how then could I look upon a virgin?" (Job 31:1).

In 1996, Americans spent more than $8 billion in pornography: hard-core videos, peep shows, adult cable programming, computer porn, and sex magazines. In 1996, Americans rented 665 million hard-core videos.[22] Allowing yourself to view such pornography is fatal to your marriage and your eternal well-being.

Pornography is not the only threat to men and their families. Fathers should be extremely cautious of both programs and *advertising* that are sexually suggestive or explicit. Forty years ago, if someone exposed children to what is shown routinely on prime time television today, he would have been thrown in jail. Our sensitivities to immoral programming have been thoroughly numbed in just one generation. Don't allow your family to participate in television's moral freefall. Some of the strongest condemnations in the New Testament come from Jesus against those who scandalize children.

> *"Whoever receives one such child in my name receives me; but whoever causes one of these little ones who believe in me to sin, it would be better for him to have a great millstone fastened round his neck and to be drowned in the depth of the sea. Woe to the world for temptations to sin! For it is necessary that temptations come, but woe to the man by whom the temptation comes!"* (Matthew 18:5-7).

Consider pasting this verse on your television set: "I will walk with integrity of heart within my house; I will not set before my eyes anything that is base" (Psalm 101:2-3).

Protecting Yourself and Your Children from Sex on the Internet

Sex is the most popular topic on the Internet. New, depraved oceans of smut are just a few mouse clicks away from your children. If you have an Internet connection in your home, then install "blocking" software on your home computer.[23] Protective software not only blocks sexually explicit sites, but it also provides an unalterable record of blocked sites that were attempted. Another excellent precaution is to place computers with access to the Internet in an open location in your home.

Many Christian men ask, "What's wrong with looking at sexy pictures on the Internet?"[24] Plenty. St. Peter warns that inflaming sexual passions corrupts your Christian life and wages war against your soul. "Beloved, I beseech you as aliens and exiles to abstain from the passions of the flesh that wage war against your soul" (1 Peter 2:11). If you are having trouble avoiding the temptations of the Internet, take the same steps to protect yourself as you do for your children.

Guardians of Our Children

The besetting sin of the twentieth century is sexual sin in all its forms. It is the door through which countless thousands have fallen away from the faith. The sexual revolution is the fuel propelling the abortion juggernaut. Once culturally accepted, sexual sin carries with it the power to darken entire societies.

Our hope for the future rests upon protecting our children's generation. However, as we protect our children from that which disturbs and corrupts their childhood innocence, we need to constantly lead by example and protect ourselves.

St. Joseph put the physical welfare of Jesus before even his job, home, friends, and convenience. As fathers following the "Guardian of the Redeemer," can we do any less when the eternal welfare of our children is at stake?

A Special Reminder to Protect the Fatherless

As Christian fathers, we are ultimately modeling our fatherhood on the fatherhood of God. In a world where over forty million children are killed annually by abortion, we must remember that God is a father to the fatherless.[25] Besides protecting his own children, Christian fathers are called to help protect the unborn babies loved by God and yet threatened by abortion.[26]

God is also father to the poor. That means that like the patriarch Job in the Old Testament we are to be fathers in assisting the poor, the widows, and the fatherless (Job 29:12, 16). As our nation becomes increasingly fatherless over the next several decades, grandfathers are going to be challenged with the task of protecting and helping to provide for their grown single-parent daughters and their fatherless grandchildren.

Commitment Seven:

Providing for Our Families

As fathers, we will assume the primary responsibility for the financial provision of our families. We will seek to learn and to apply Christian principles of financial stewardship within our families. Whenever possible, we will seek to provide the maximum opportunity for our wives to nurture our children at home.

Providing for Our Families

"Pray then like this: 'Our Father who art in heaven.... Give us this day our daily bread.'"
—Matthew 6:9, 11

"Honor the LORD with your substance and with the first fruits of all your produce; then your barns will be filled with plenty, and your vats will be bursting with wine."
—Proverbs 3:9-10

I stood at the kitchen window staring at my backyard and agonizing over how the Family Life Center was going to survive financially. In the year after founding St. Joseph's Covenant Keepers we experienced a 1,200 percent growth in the families in our network, but only a 4 percent growth in donations. Our success was killing us financially. We only had a few days of operating funds left. Since we did not even have the money to send a mailing to our supporters notifying them of our predicament, I was facing the prospect of closing our doors and having no job. While transfixed on these financial anxieties, I felt a little tug on my leg.

I looked down to see my two-year-old daughter, Susan, holding a cup and asking me for a drink of water before bedtime. Her eyes reflected a special childlike confidence; there was not a hint of doubt or anxiety in her request. She simply trusted me to fulfill her need. As I handed Susan back her cup of water I wondered why I couldn't trust God for my needs the same way my daughter trusted me. Didn't

Jesus say that instead of financial anxieties we were to have confidence in our heavenly Father?

> *"Therefore do not be anxious, saying, 'What shall we eat?' or 'What shall we drink?' or 'What shall we wear?' For the Gentiles seek all these things; and your heavenly Father knows that you need them all. But seek first his kingdom and his righteousness, and all these things shall be yours as well. Therefore do not be anxious about tomorrow, for tomorrow will be anxious for itself. Let the day's own trouble be sufficient for the day"* (Matthew 6:31-34).

Knowing that we should trust our heavenly Father instead of having financial anxieties is one thing. Actually doing it in trying circumstances is something else, especially for grown-ups like me with little faith!

I was still at the window when it hit me that St. Joseph could be the missing link between a doubting, anxiety-filled father and our heavenly Father. Certainly St. Joseph can relate to family financial anxieties. He was a man of modest means who received a midnight job transfer from an angel. Overnight he had to pack up and leave his homeland. St. Joseph faced the challenge of providing for his uprooted family in a foreign country with just a few of his carpenter's tools.

St. Joseph is better than a friend who can merely relate to our financial difficulties; he can do something about it! James 5:16 says, "the prayer of a righteous man has great power in its effects." Matthew 1:19 calls Joseph the "just man." The two English terms "just man" and "righteous man" are two ways to translate the same core Greek word. Therefore, St. Joseph is the righteous man with unique intercessory access to God himself. In the carpenter shop Jesus willingly responded to any request by St. Joseph. Do you think that Jesus responds any differently to a request that St. Joseph would make on our behalf today?

Go to Joseph!

In the Old Testament era, when both pagan and Jewish people needed "daily bread" during an excruciating famine, they were told, "go to Joseph" (Genesis 41:55). God raised up the patriarch Joseph to provide for the needs of many in the midst of great want. The Church Fathers taught that the Old Testament patriarch Joseph foreshadowed St. Joseph in the New Testament. Contemporary fathers struggling to provide "daily bread" for their families need to "go to Joseph." In St. Joseph they will find a powerful and sympathetic advocate.

In a renewed way, I entrusted my family's finances and the work of the Family Life Center to St. Joseph that evening. I asked him to carry and present our needs to God. Within a week we were out of financial danger. Within a month we were back on our feet financially. Incredible! Through this and subsequent experiences I have learned that St. Joseph is a saint that fathers can rely upon when the chips are down. You don't "go to Joseph" and come away disappointed.

God the Father gave Jesus a perfect earthly father to provide for his needs. Because Jesus is our brother through the New Covenant (Hebrews 2:11-12), we share both his fathers: his heavenly Father as well as his human father, St. Joseph. When we need an intercessor for our daily bread with the Heavenly Father, St. Joseph stands willing to help any father who asks for his assistance.[1]

The Need to Support Families with Financial Struggles

Financial anxiety has almost become a way of life for many modern families. A recent poll revealed that a third of all adults in the United States have trouble sleeping or relaxing because of financial anxieties.[2]

Too often, many of these families struggling financially sense little or no support from the Church. Listen to the anguish of a father from Stamford, Connecticut:

As someone who was "restructured"—that is, fired—from his job in 1983, I've completely lost interest in reading Catholic newspapers. I'm also finding it terribly difficult to go to Mass, since I don't hear a word of understanding there for those of us living a financial nightmare.

When I wrote Pope John Paul II about the sufferings of American children due to unemployment, the Holy Father acknowledged my letter and said he would pray for me and my family at Mass. He understood the sufferings many are going through.

But the lack of understanding in Catholic newspapers and in the Catholic community as a whole is demoralizing. I get the sense that my sufferings aren't worth noting or addressing.[3]

The Importance of Praying for Family Finances

Families should respectfully request that prayers be offered during Mass, not only for the poor, but also for all struggling families, businesses, workers, salesmen, and those needing jobs. After seven years as a Catholic I cannot remember hearing a single prayer during Mass on behalf of the finances for middle-class families. Someone like the father writing from Connecticut could easily get the impression that the Church is neither aware of nor cares about the enormous financial pressures faced by average families today.

> *Have no anxiety about anything, but in everything by prayer and supplication with thanksgiving let your requests be made known to God. And the peace of God, which passes all understanding, will keep your hearts and your minds in Christ Jesus* (Philippians 4:6-7).

A regular feature of Christian men's groups should be mutual prayer for family finances. Encourage children to pray for the success of the family breadwinners. Promote devotion and intercessory prayer to St. Joseph as a way of relieving some of the financial stresses faced by families. Share answered prayers with congregations, small groups, and families as a way of inviting others to discover that God is willing to be the Father of their family's finances.

The Importance of Tithing

Tithing is another way to entrust your family's finances to the care of God the Father. Just the idea of tithing seems to make many Catholics nervous. In reality, tithing is a way to *reduce* financial stress. It is the principal way to gain the assurance that our heavenly Father will provide for our needs.

> *"For I the LORD do not change; therefore you, O sons of Jacob, are not consumed. From the days of your fathers you have turned aside from my statutes and have not kept them. Return to me, and I will return to you, says the LORD of hosts. But you say, 'How shall we return?' Will man rob God? Yet you are robbing me. But you say, 'How are we robbing thee?' In your tithes and offerings.*

You are cursed with a curse, for you are robbing me; the whole nation of you. Bring the full tithes into the storehouse, that there may be food in my house; and thereby put me to the test, says the LORD of hosts, if I will not open the windows of heaven for you and pour down for you an overflowing blessing" (Malachi 3:6-10).

God is so eager to become the covenant Father of our finances that he actually invites us to test him. What makes this so remarkable is that it is usually sinful to put God to a test.[4] In Malachi 3, God reminds us that he has not changed his mind about the necessity of tithing. Furthermore, God promises that if we honor him with a full tithe, he will shower us with abundant blessings.

Tithing is giving God 10 percent of our financial increase as a sign of our recognition of his Lordship over all our wealth.[5] By tithing, we recognize that God holds the right and title to all our possessions. Further, we acknowledge that all our increase comes from his hand. In the New Covenant God fully expects to be honored as the great King of Kings with our full tithe.[6] In return, the King of Kings and Lord of Lords becomes the covenant Father of our finances to provide for our daily bread.

When tithing, Christians must not act like an Uncle Scrooge whining about having to fork over some cash. St. Paul says, "Each one must do as he has made up his mind, *not reluctantly or under compulsion, for God loves a cheerful giver"* (2 Corinthians 9:7). The original Greek word translated *cheerful* literally means *hilarious.* God loves joyful, hilarious givers who donate willingly to help the poor and to advance Christ's Kingdom.

Don't say to yourself, "I can't do it. I don't make enough money." Don't think that once you earn more that it will get easier to start tithing. Often, the more money you make, the more difficult it becomes to tithe.

Just do it! Step out in faith and start tithing for a test period of twelve months. God challenges us to put him to the test! If we believe that God has the ability to change ordinary bread into the body and blood of Christ, certainly we should believe that he can provide our daily bread. If we will honor him as Father of our finances by tithing, God promises to reward us with overwhelming blessings.

Ending the His-Versus-Hers Financial Struggle

Tithing solves the two most common money problems in families: (1) quarrels over his-versus-hers; and (2) not enough to go around.

In a marriage, whose money is it anyway: his, hers, both? The root of the his-versus-hers financial conflict is a dispute over ownership. Who rightfully owns the money in a family? God. When a couple turns 100 percent of the ownership of their wealth over to God, marital unity supplants the tug-of-war. The money is no longer his or hers, but God's. By tithing, a family formally acknowledges that God is Lord of all their possessions. As husband and wife recognize that they are merely stewards entrusted with God's wealth, the tension turns into teamwork.

> *But those who desire to be rich fall into temptation, into a snare, into many senseless and hurtful desires that plunge men into ruin and destruction. For the love of money is the root of all evils; it is through this craving that some have wandered away from the faith and pierced their hearts with many pangs* (1 Timothy 6:9-10).

Don't underestimate the power of money over our hearts. The Bob Dylan song was right: "You Gotta Serve Somebody." We cannot serve both the Almighty Dollar and the Almighty Lord (Matthew 6:24). We will either honor God as Lord of our money or honor money as lord of our lives. Love of money displaces love of God and snuffs out charity for spouse and children. God wants us to make a good living for our families, but a not a financial killing that destroys our homes. All men—rich, poor, or in-between—need to guard against a fixation on money and material possessions. "And as for what fell among the thorns, they are those who hear [the Word of God], but as they go on their way they are choked by the cares and riches and pleasures of life, and their fruit does not mature" (Luke 8:14).

While tithing is not a financial cure-all, it is an indispensable first step in the path to financial freedom. A practical way to keep God first in our family finances is to make the tithe the first item in the family budget and to pay the tithe before paying the monthly bills.

Finding Enough Money for Your Needs

Scripture promises that those who tithe will have enough money to meet their financial needs. "Honor the LORD with your substance and with the first fruits of all your produce; then your barns will be filled with plenty, and your vats will be bursting with wine" (Proverbs 3:9-10).

However, it is a misconception to think of tithing as some type of divine get-rich-quick scheme. God does promise economic abundance, but not automatic wealth. Tithing is not a magic money multiplier. Christian stewardship involves preparation, education, hard work, service, perseverance, thrift, and generosity. Attempting to get rich quickly does not fit into the Christian plan for family finances. Tithing often results in increased income to meet family needs. However, the blessings of tithing frequently come indirectly as well.

Some of the indirect blessings of tithing include: peace of heart knowing that God is actively caring for your family's finances, contentment with your financial condition, an increase of charity toward God and neighbor, wisdom for making good investment and business decisions, the common sense to avoid get-rich-quick schemes, and self-control to resist the allures of consumer debt.

Escaping Consumer Debt

The greatest avoidable drain upon family finances is consumer debt. Debt is a form of economic bondage. In my experience, the families that find the wisdom and the fortitude necessary to decrease and to eventually eliminate their debt load are usually the same families who practice tithing. Placing your family's finances under the Lordship of Christ through tithing is the door to economic liberation. Families walking this path will discover financial freedom as they escape the quicksand of never-ending debt.[7]

It's amazing how a little piece of plastic can enslave a family's finances and even ruin a marriage. Credit card debt in 1996 reached 400 billion dollars. The average American family carries a month to month balance on their credit cards of $4,000.[8] No wonder financial problems repeatedly surface as a major cause of divorce. Eliminating consumer debt liberates a family from spiraling monthly payments. Instead of making your creditors rich, you can begin saving for your family's future. Being debt-free also minimizes the agony of being unexpectedly laid-off, or undergoing an economic reversal.

Who is the real master when you float debt on your credit cards? Are we really mastering the moment by piling up debt, or is the moment mastering us? Listen to Proverbs 22:7, which is sometimes called the "master card" verse of the Bible: "The rich rules over the poor, and the borrower is the slave of the lender."

Giving Our Wives the Maximum Opportunity to Nurture Our Children

During election seasons, candidates from all political parties promise tax relief for families with children. What type of substantial changes should they make? A good start would be increasing the federal tax exemption for dependents. Adjusting for inflation, the buying power of the 1948 personal exemption on federal taxes would be over $6,000 per person today.[9] This one change would give millions of mothers the opportunity to stay home with their children. Before you say that such an exemption is too expensive, ask yourself, "Why should mothers be forced from the presence of their children in order to make payments to the Internal Revenue Service?"

Pope John Paul II has said that one of the most pressing concerns facing modern families and economies is mothers who are forced to work outside the home.

> Dealing with the relationship between the family and the economy, you cannot fail to face the question of the work of women outside the home. The issue today is generally not the right of women to enter the work-force or to follow a career. The pressing question is that of finding ways for working wives and mothers to carry out their irreplaceable service within the family....[10]

Starting in World War II and accelerating through the sixties, women poured into the work force. By the mid-1990s, however, a surprising counter-migration had begun. In 1994, *Barron's* financial newspaper reported the beginning of a "demographic sea change" silently taking place in the labor force. "The traditional one-paycheck family is now the fastest growing household unit."[11] More and more women are leaving the workplace in order to nurture their children at home.

Modern technology is allowing wives to provide a significant contribution to the family's financial welfare while working from the home.[12] The growth of home-based business opportunities is good news to the many women who need to work and yet want to be at home with their children. With a home-based business there can be a two-paycheck family with a stay-at-home mom.

Challenges in Providing for Your Family

The traditional role of a father includes the solemn responsibility to be the family's primary breadwinner. In the face of financial pressures, many Christian men today are challenged by the exhortation in 1 Timothy 5:8: "If any one does not provide for his relatives, and especially for his own family, he has disowned the faith and is worse than an unbeliever."

Ironically, in the midst of America's economic abundance, fathers are finding it harder to make a decent living. Nearly a third of American men aged twenty-five to thirty-four do not earn enough to keep a family with two children above the poverty line.[13] The idea of a "family wage," compensation sufficient to support a family and varying according to family size, has disappeared.

Not only has our economy failed fathers, but increasingly, fathers are failing their families. Between 1957 and 1976, the percentage of fathers who considered providing for their children as one of their life goals dropped by more than half.[14] During this same period the number of working men who viewed marriage and children as "burdensome and restrictive" more than doubled.[15]

In many families, the wife can earn more money than her husband. Some couples in this situation are deciding that the husband should stay at home while the wife becomes the primary bread-winner. Working moms and stay-at-home dads is not a wise, long-term arrangement. "There is wrath and impudence and great disgrace when a wife supports her husband" (Sirach [Ecclesiasticus] 25:22). Rather than reversing the roles that have guided families since the dawn of history, it would be wiser to seek training or opportunities to boost the husband's earning potential.

Mothers Are the Heart of the Home

Since this book is about Christian fatherhood we have strongly emphasized the irreplaceable role of fathers in the family. Yet we also
want to accentuate the crowning role of mothers as the very heart of
the family.[16] From a mother's heart pours forth the charity that makes
family life the most loving circle on earth. There is no person, place,
or thing that can replace the constant stream of a mother's love and
care. Children have an insatiable appetite for a mother's nurturing
love. One of the best things a father can ever do for his children is to
provide the maximum opportunity for their mother to nurture them
at home.

Commitment Eight:

Building Our Marriages and Families on the "Rock"

As St. Joseph's Covenant Keepers, we will seek to build our homes on the "Rock" by following the teachings of the successors of St. Peter. We will seek to learn and to live by the historically rooted Church teachings on marriage, family, and human sexuality. This includes the Church's teaching on birth control. Those who practice the Church's teaching have a divorce rate of less than 5 percent. Those who are following the creator's plan for marriage are discovering a powerful strengthening of their marriages. Conversely, a skyrocketing divorce rate has closely paralleled the ignoring of Church teaching.

Building Our Marriages and Families on the "Rock"

"Every one then who hears these words of mine and does them will be like a wise man who built his house upon the rock; and the rain fell, and the floods came, and the winds blew and beat upon that house, but it did not fall, because it had been founded on the rock. And every one who hears these words of mine and does not do them will be like a foolish man who built his house upon the sand; and the rain fell, and the floods came, and the winds blew and beat against that house, and it fell; and great was the fall of it."
—Matthew 7:24-27

"And I tell you, you are Peter [Rock], and on this rock I will build my church, and the powers of death [Hades] shall not prevail against it."
—Matthew 16:18

In August, 1992, the most expensive natural disaster in U.S. history was heading toward my home state of Florida. Although the National Hurricane Center had alerted us that a killer hurricane was on the way, many Floridians made the costly mistake of ignoring the storm warnings for Hurricane Andrew.

Packing winds up to 200 mph, Hurricane Andrew cut a ruinous swath across South Florida on August 25, flattening houses and toppling palm trees, causing approximately $25 billion in damages. The ferocious storm left twenty-three people dead and nearly a quarter of a million people homeless.

Hurricane Andrew virtually wiped the town of Homestead, Florida off the map. One Internet report described the hurricane's carnage in Homestead:

> Destruction reigned until barely anything was left upright. By dawn, Homestead looked as though someone had turned a blender on it—and forgotten the lid. The town of 32,000 was shredded and tossed about. Telephone poles were snapped in two. Roofs were peeled away, balconies were unhinged, and fences were ripped down.

The next day, the quiet town of Homestead looked like a war zone. Many residents returned to find their homes blown apart. In some areas, the hurricane's destruction was so complete that owners couldn't even identify the lots on which their homes had once stood.

Unlike California where earthquakes can occur at any moment, in Florida we at least get warnings for our chief natural disasters. Unfortunately, warnings from the National Hurricane Center won't help if they aren't heeded.

Storm Warnings from the Vatican

For more than a century the Vatican has been a type of National Hurricane Center for the killer storm raging against families. Starting with the prophetic warnings of Pope Leo XIII in the late nineteenth century, there have been five distinct severe storm alerts for the modern family:

- Leo XIII, *Christian Marriage* [*Arcanum Divinae*], 1880.
- Pius XI, *Christian Marriage* [*Casti Connubii*], 1930.
- Paul VI, *Of Human Life* [*Humanae Vitae*], 1968.
- John Paul II, *The Role of the Christian Family in the Modern World* [*Familiaris Consortio*], 1981.
- John Paul II, *Letter to Families*, 1994.[1]

Something far more powerful than the common pressures of contemporary life energizes the storm against modern families. This assault against the family has a supernatural dimension. As St. Paul said, "We are not contending against flesh and blood, but against the principalities, against the powers, against the world rulers of this present darkness, against the spiritual hosts of wickedness in the heavenly places" (Ephesians 6:12).

Satan's Century?

After celebrating Mass at the Vatican on October 13, 1884, Pope Leo XIII stood motionless for several minutes as he was allowed to overhear a conversation between God and Satan. This dialogue sounded similar to the exchange in the beginning of the book of Job where Satan asks God for permission to subject Job to a period of severe testing.

Pope Leo heard Satan boast that he could destroy the Church if he just had adequate power and a century to accomplish the task. Divine providence allows the Church to be tested just as Jesus and Job passed through a time of trial.[2] God granted Satan his request with the understanding that if the devil's plan failed he would suffer a crushing defeat.[3]

During his vision, the Pope also saw St. Michael the Archangel casting Satan and his demons into hell. Immediately after this terrifying experience, Pope Leo XIII went to his chambers and composed the prayer to St. Michael the Archangel.[4]

Satan's Strategy for Destroying the Faith and the Family

Sexual sin has been one of Satan's primary ploys for destroying the faith and the family throughout history, especially during the twentieth century. Satan's time-proven strategy to deceive the faithful and to destroy the Church is to have "all nations drink the wine of ... impure passion" (Revelation 14:8). He uses the "passions of the flesh" to wage war against our souls (1 Peter 2:11). Satan knows that sexual immorality "increases the faithless among men" (Proverbs 23:28) and that a "strong delusion" descends over those who have "pleasure in unrighteousness" (2 Thessalonians 2:11-12). Satan knows better than most of us the tragic darkening of the mind to truth that follows the social acceptance of sexual impurities and unnatural relations (Romans 1:18-32).

The pivotal cause of the sexual revolution and its resulting family disintegration is the seemingly harmless use of birth control. The popes of this century have known hell's cunning scheme to corrupt marriages by corrupting marital sexuality. They have foreseen and predicted with stunning clarity the painful consequences to family life that would accompany the acceptance of artificial contraception.

Pope Paul VI's famous encyclical, *Humanae Vitae* [*Of Human Life*], has become the moral dividing line of the twentieth century. Written in 1968, *Humanae Vitae* repeated the Church's unchangeable condemnation of artificial birth control, abortion, and sterilization. No papal encyclical in Christian history has met with such widespread public dissent by both clergy and laity.

Drawn by the Splendor of Truth

Paradoxically, many Protestants have been drawn to the Catholic Church precisely because of her unyielding fidelity to the timeless Christian teaching on birth control. I am one of them. Listen to the testimony of Malcolm Muggeridge, the late BBC commentator who converted to Catholicism before his death:

> As a non-Catholic, as an aspiring Christian, as someone who, as an old journalist, has watched this process of deterioration in our whole way of life; what I want to say is that in the encyclical [*Humanae Vitae*] the finger is pointed on the point that really matters. Namely, that through human procreation the great creativity of men and women comes into play, and that to interfere with this creativity, to seek to relate it merely to pleasure, is to go back into pre-Christian times and ultimately to destroy the civilization that Christianity has brought about. If there is one thing I feel *absolutely certain* about, it is that. One thing that I know will appear in social histories in the future is that the dissolution of our way of life, our Christian way of life and all that it has meant to the world, relates directly to the matter that is raised in *Humanae Vitae*.[5]

Unanimously Condemned by Christianity

Today most people think that opposition to birth control is just a Catholic issue. It hasn't always been that way.

Until 1930, every denomination of the Christian Church in every century of her existence condemned artificial contraception. Every major Protestant leader condemned birth control. John Calvin compared birth control to "a violent abortion," calling it "a crime incapable of expiation;" Martin Luther viewed it as sodomy and called those who practiced it "swinish monsters;" and John Wesley warned that those engaging in such perverse actions "destroy their own souls."[6]

Margaret Sanger, the founder of the Birth Control League (later to become Planned Parenthood) mounted a successful campaign to persuade the Church of England to accept artificial birth control in 1930. The Anglicans were not alone in their doctrinal reversal. Over the next few decades, other Protestant denominations fell like dominoes in allowing birth control. By the time the pill was introduced in the 1960s, birth control and sterilization were viewed as morally acceptable and culturally desirable by almost everyone but faithful Catholics.

What is Causing the Explosion of Divorce?

Is it just a coincidence that the greatest havoc in Christian marriages in history has accompanied the acceptance of birth control? Since Margaret Sanger introduced artificial birth control in the United States in 1916, the divorce rate has increased by 500 percent. Since the introduction of the pill in the 1960s, the divorce rate has doubled. The current divorce rate for new marriages is about 50 percent. The correlation between the spread of birth control and the spread of divorce is not just a matter of chance when you consider that those following the Church's teaching and avoiding all forms of artificial birth control have a divorce rate under 5 percent.[7]

Why does avoiding birth control cause the divorce rate to plummet from 50 percent to less than 5 percent? Why would accepting or avoiding artificial birth control make such a drastic difference in the strength of the marriage bond?

The twentieth century is closing with millions of men, women, and especially, children suffering from the excruciating pain of divorce. They are the walking wounded, their hearts and souls punctured by broken marriages. Those who have been divorced along with those who fear being divorced are searching for ways to strengthen marriages and cure the crippling epidemic of marital dissolution.

Our whole society is longing to know the secret to having a lifelong, loving marriage.

Who Is the Real Love Expert?

Desperate couples devour books and tapes, seeking help for their marriages. In 1994, Americans spent twenty-six million dollars for a tape set by best-selling author Barbara De Angelis called *Making Love Work*. Interestingly enough, this popular love expert has been divorced *four* times, including a divorce from another popular love expert, John Gray, author of the best-selling book, *Men Are From Mars, Women Are From Venus*. However, this has not deterred spouses from spending millions in hopes of discovering the secret glue for holding marriages together.

Sadly, countless couples are rejecting the very solution that will satisfy their deepest desire. *Humanae Vitae*, the moral teaching that couples are rejecting most, contains the secret to the strong marriage that couples are seeking most. Although it sounds unbelievable, *Humanae Vitae* is a 75-cent cure for the ravenous cancer eating at the heart of marriages. This remarkable remedy can even be free if you have access to the Internet.[8]

A few years ago, I was riding with a trucker the day after John Paul II publicly reaffirmed the Church's teaching against birth control. When he heard the pope mentioned on the radio, the driver exploded with a string of expletives and a sarcastic snarl, "What the * * * * * does that old pope know about sex, anyway?" While this may come as a big surprise to that truck driver, Pope John Paul II knows approximately ten thousand times more about marital sexuality than the average American male, including the so-called love experts.

What is the Secret to Marital Sexuality?

What do the popes in Rome know about marital sexuality that most men in our sex-saturated society don't? Papal encyclicals, letters, and exhortations have repeatedly taught that sex isn't just something that people "do." God designed the marital embrace to cause a profound union of persons and a deep renewal of the marriage covenant. The *Catechism of the Catholic Church* says,

> Sexuality, by means which man and woman give themselves to one another through the acts which are proper and exclusive to spouses, is not something simply biological, but concerns the innermost being of the human person....[9]

This joining of persons, not just bodies, is at the heart of the mystery of the marital embrace. The Old Testament word for the marital union is the Hebrew verb "to know."[10] It is significant that this verb is never used to describe animal copulation. Marital sexuality is not just a biological act, as it is among animals; it is a conscious, personal union that completely unites a man and a woman.[11] A husband and wife are not two solitary individuals who happen to live under the same roof. Rather, they have entered a mysterious oneness in their marriage covenant. By God's design, a couple's marriage covenant experiences a deep renewal of its oneness every time their sexual embrace includes a total self-giving.[12]

> Every man and every woman fully realizes himself or herself through the sincere gift of self. For spouses, the moment of conjugal union constitutes a very particular expression of this. It is then that a man and woman, in the 'truth' of their masculinity and femininity, become a mutual gift to each other. All married life is a gift; but this becomes most evident when the spouses, in giving themselves to each other in love, bring about that encounter which makes them 'one flesh' (Genesis 2:24).[13]

Keeping Selfishness Out of Your Marriage Bed

The essence of love is self-giving. The opposite of genuine love is selfishness. Using artificial birth control is inherently selfish because one seeks the pleasure of the sexual union while withholding the procreative part of oneself. The language of marital love says, "I give you all of myself; I accept all of you." The language of contraceptive sex says, "I give you all of myself, except my fertility; I accept all of you, except your life-giving part." Instead of mutual self-*giving*, contraception implies mutual self-*reservation*. The very act which God designed to strengthen and renew the marriage covenant is subtly corrupted into an act of profound selfishness. Habitual stinginess in the hearts of spouses inevitably creates friction in the marriage. This perverted self-reservation too often escalates into an unyielding conflict of the wills and ends up in a divorce court. Frequently, the couple won't have any idea what really destroyed their marriage.

Acts Against Nature

It is an act against nature and gravely immoral to separate *love-making* (the unitive—Genesis 2:24) from *baby-making* (the procreative—Genesis 1:28). Artificial birth control is gravely sinful because it unnaturally frustrates the procreative part of the marriage act. The new *Catechism of the Catholic Church* teaches:

> each and every marriage act must remain open to the transmission of life.... This particular doctrine, expounded on numerous occasions by the Magisterium, is based on the inseparable connection, established by God, which man on his own initiative may not break, between the unitive and procreative significance which are both inherent in the marriage act.[14]

Any sexual activity that separates the procreative purpose from the unitive purpose is gravely sinful. This includes masturbation, homosexual acts, sterilization (vasectomies or tubal ligations), devices to prevent conception, and acts consciously intended to interrupt coitus and thwart procreation.[15]

How does God react to those who separate the two ends of marriage? For such a willful act against the nature of the sex act, one man in the Old Testament paid with his life.

> *Then Judah said to Onan, "Go in to your brother's wife, and perform the duty of a brother-in-law to her, and raise up offspring for your brother." But Onan knew that the offspring would not be his; so when he went in to his brother's wife he spilled the semen on the ground, lest he should give offspring to his brother. And what he did was displeasing in the sight of the LORD, and he slew him also* (Genesis 38:8-10).

To be fair, I should mention that there is a flood of contemporary Christian family experts, scripture scholars, theologians, and preachers, who say that Onan was not killed for spilling his semen, but for disobeying God's command to continue his brother's family name. You will find that this same group generally sees nothing terribly wrong with masturbation and the use of artificial birth control.

Yet, the uniform voice of Protestant and Catholic leaders in former generations interpreted Onan's act of spilling his seed as worthy of eternal damnation.[16] Martin Luther said, "That was a sin [Onan's] far greater than adultery or incest, and it provoked God to such fierce wrath that He destroyed him immediately."[17] For twenty centuries Catholic teaching has seen this passage as a solemn warning not to frustrate the procreative end of the marital embrace.

Freud's Definition of Sexual Perversions

Even Sigmund Freud, who was never a friend of Christianity, said that sexual perversions are defined by their willful frustration of the procreative purpose of the sex act:

> It is a characteristic common to all the perversions that in them reproduction as an aim is put aside. This is actually the criterion by which we judge whether a sexual activity is perverse—if it departs from reproduction in its aims and pursues the attainment of gratification independently.[18]

Regulating Birth Without Offending Moral Principles

Does all this mean that spouses must have a baby every time they enjoy marital relations? Of course not. God has generously given spouses both fertile and infertile times to renew their marriage bond. God doesn't insist that sex occur only during the fertile times. But God does insist that if spouses choose to use the fertile time for bonding, that they remain open to babies. For couples who have serious reasons for avoiding or postponing pregnancy, it is perfectly moral to have marital relations only during the wife's infertile times.

> If, then, there are serious motives to space out births, which derive from the physical or psychological conditions of husband and wife, or from external conditions, the Church teaches that it is then licit to take into account the natural rhythms immanent in the generative functions, for the use of marriage in the infecund [infertile] periods only, and in this way to regulate birth without offending the moral principles which have been recalled earlier.[19]

This natural method of spacing births is called Natural Family Planning. It should not be confused with the unreliable calendar rhythm method developed in the 1930s. Natural Family Planning can be used to aid couples both in achieving pregnancy and in avoiding pregnancy where serious reasons exist for doing so. The method effectiveness for avoiding pregnancy with Natural Family Planning is 99 percent,[20] which is greater than the most effective artificial contraceptive.

Isn't using Natural Family Planning just the same as using chemicals or devices to avoid pregnancy? Again, no. "There are essential differences between the two cases; in the former, the married couple make legitimate use of a natural disposition; in the latter, they impede the development of natural processes."[21] For example, two men might both want to lose weight. One exercises self-discipline and eats less. The other eats whatever he wants and then forces himself to vomit. They both have the same goal, but one uses natural means and the other unnatural means to attain it. When used with the right motives, Natural Family Planning is in complete harmony with God's design in nature and with the moral law.

Enlarging Our Hearts to Receive God's Blessings

Doesn't the Church require married couples to have babies? No, it is a common misconception that the Catholic Church somehow forces couples to have children. It has never forced and will never compel anyone to conceive a child. Yet, Christian couples are not free to arrive at their decisions in an autonomous fashion. In every area of Christian living, we must make decisions with minds conformed to truth. Anything less than this would be something less than a truly Christian decision.

Therefore, the Church exhorts couples to conform their consciences to the intentions of God in making decisions about family size. The Church, expressing God's love for children, encourages couples to be generous in the service of life.[22] What exactly does being "generous" mean? For most of us it will mean that we allow God the opportunity to enlarge our hearts so we can fully submit to his purposes for our lives. Often our hearts are too small to contain God's blessings.

What does God desire from our marriage covenants? Godly children. The prophet Malachi said, "the LORD was witness to the covenant between you and the wife of your youth.... Has not the one God made and sustained for us the spirit of life? And what does he desire? Godly offspring" (Malachi 2:14-15).

Christ's own disciples thought that his ministry was too important to bother him with children. Parents considering family size need to hear afresh Jesus' response to his disciples: "Let the children come to me, and do not hinder them; for to such belongs the kingdom of heaven" (Matthew 19:14).

Christian couples are called to imitate the generosity and fruitfulness of our heavenly Father. Are you and your wife willing to prayerfully ask God to give both of you the desire to have at least one more child if that is his will? Are you willing to ask God for the desire to welcome as many children as he wants to send you? God is capable of changing your minds and filling your hearts with desires to conform to his will—if you simply ask him. "For God is at work in you, both to will and to work for his good pleasure" (Philippians 2:13).

In his *Letter to Families*, Pope John Paul II encouraged couples to focus their prayers on childbearing:

> Should our prayer not concentrate on the crucial and decisive moment of the passage from conjugal love to childbearing, and thus to fatherhood and motherhood? Is that not precisely the moment when there is an indispensable need for the 'outpouring of the grace of the Holy Spirit'...?[23]

What happens when we invite God to expand our hearts and conform our will to his in the area of family planning? Frequently, the result is babies. I have held newborns in my arms ten months after some Christian couples took sixty seconds to pray such a prayer. The glow from the faces of the parents showed that conformity to our heavenly Father's will brings fulfillment beyond the ability of language to express.

What Is Our Attitude Toward Children?

We have arrived at the crucial question facing fathers in the modern world: what is our attitude toward children, especially having more of our own children? Are children a disease so that we must protect ourselves from catching one? Are they a cancer that we must mutilate ourselves to be rid of them? Or are they the crowning fruit of married love and the greatest blessing God can bestow on a couple?[24]

A deeply rooted anti-child mentality grows alongside the acceptance of artificial birth control. This anti-child mentality is a poisoned arrow aimed directly at the heart of fatherhood. It turns the hearts of fathers away from even the desire to have children. It is the very opposite of the turning of the hearts of fathers toward their children described in Malachi 4:6. Birth control's anti-child mentality is a strike against fatherhood itself.

The essence of fatherhood is having children, either through physical generation or adoption.[25] The new catechism says that spouses are called to give life and thereby "share in the creative power and fatherhood of God. By giving life, spouses participate in God's fatherhood."[26] This is the soul of fruitful fatherhood and married life.

Recall our "report card" in chapter three which evaluated any Christian men's movement by the standard of lasting fruit (John 15:16). Children are not just a fruit of the marriage covenant, they are the *eternal fruit* of a marriage. "Let all be convinced that human life and the duty of transmitting it are not limited by the horizons of this life only: their true evaluation and full significance can be understood only in reference to *man's eternal destiny*."[27]

The Pivot of Civilization

Pope John Paul II has said that the "future of civilization is directly dependent upon the issue of responsible motherhood and fatherhood."[28] This is the pivot of civilization. As long as the plague of birth control continues to infect marriages with selfishness, we will face a destructive anti-civilization.[29] As long as we remain addicted to the anti-child mentality of contraception, the culture of death will haunt us. Only by recovering a fruitful family life can we recover a civilization of love.

God is showering us with an unusual outpouring of the Holy Spirit. During a season of renewal, God's grace is abundantly available to regenerate hearts and change lives. His grace is strong enough to melt even the hardest of hearts. It is powerful enough to cut through rebellious dissent from Church teaching. It is powerful enough to conquer the sin of artificial birth control. It is even powerful enough to turn fathers' hearts toward having children.

Scuttle the Eighth Commitment?

Will the contemporary Christian men's movement seize the moment before us, or will we squander this once-in-a-lifetime opportunity? Obviously, it would be easier to scuttle the eighth commitment to attract more members. But if we keep quiet about birth control, we will be building on sand. We cannot measure our success by an immediate growth in numbers, but by fruit that endures for generations.

The quick road to success is always alluring. The devil in the desert offered Jesus sensational shortcuts, but he rejected them.[30] So should we. Eliminating the eighth commitment of St. Joseph's Covenant Keepers would doom us to be a one generation phenomenon, a passing fad. Any Christian men's group that fails to address the birth-control issue will be impotent to revitalize the family. Cutting off the eighth commitment helps perpetuate birth control's corruption of the heart of fatherhood and its sacrilegious perversion of the holy sacrament of Matrimony.

Withstanding the Storm Against the Family

If current trends continue, by the year 2000 the majority of American families with children will not have a father living in the home.[31] For a preview of where our society is heading look at many of our inner cities where fatherlessness has already become the norm. It is not a pretty sight.

Over the next two decades, we will undoubtedly see a flood of programs designed to stop the disintegration of marriage and family life. These halfway remedies will not be effective. We will see a continuing devastation of family life until we return to the one and only foundation capable of withstanding the storm against the modern family, the historic Christian Faith.

Fatherlessness and family breakdown will continue until family life is again built upon the rock-solid foundation of the successors of St. Peter. Jesus said that Peter would be an immovable rock, even when blasted by the full powers of hell. This promise to St. Peter applies to his successors, the popes down through the centuries.[32] The survival of the modern family is going to require nothing less than a faithful adherence to the fullness of historic Christian teaching on marriage and family life.

Habitat for Humanity, 27, Hurricane Andrew, 0

When Hurricane Andrew's twenty-five billion dollar storm hit Dade County, Florida in 1992, twenty-seven of the most economical homes in the county survived the devastation. Interestingly, Habitat for Humanity built all these homes. This organization builds homes for low-income families with volunteer labor. They also use hammers and nails on the roofs instead of staple guns. Hurricane Andrew revealed that Habitat for Humanity had built their homes the smart way.

I live on the west coast of Florida opposite Dade County. Can you guess what the editorial page in my local paper suggested? They thought it would be wise if our county drafted building codes to emulate the "old-fashioned" building methods of Habitat for Humanity.

Building Your House on the "Rock"

Jesus spoke of two houses, built on different foundations, having two radically different outcomes after being hit by an intense storm:

> *"Every one then who hears these words of mine and does them will be like a wise man who built his house upon the rock; and the rain fell, and the floods came, and the winds blew and beat upon that house, but it did not fall, because it had been founded on the rock. And every one who hears these words of mine and does not do them will be like a foolish man who built his house upon the sand; and the rain fell, and the floods came, and the winds blew and beat against that house, and it fell; and great was the fall of it"* (Matthew 7:24-27).

Like the wise man in Matthew 7, Jesus explicitly builds his house, the Church, on a rock. "And I tell you, you are Peter [Rock], and on this rock I will build my church, and the powers of death [Hades] shall not prevail against it" (Matthew 16:18). If we want to preserve our families from the powers of hell, we should build them on the sure teachings of the Rock's successors, the popes down to the present day.

As St. Joseph's Covenant Keepers, we are committed to building our families on the Rock of St. Peter and his successors. We will build our families upon the marital and family teaching preserved by the Catholic Church through the centuries, paying special attention to the five papal documents mentioned at the beginning of this chapter. Heeding these papal storm warnings might seem like an old-fashioned Catholic notion without any modern relevance. Just wait. The storm against the family is far from over. The next few decades will fully expose the instability of any other foundation for the contemporary family.

A Closing Challenge to Christian Fathers

The prospect of being a father during the greatest whirlwind of family dissolution in recorded history can seem overwhelming. Yet, we can have a quiet confidence in the midst of the storm because Jesus has promised to be with us. We know that his promises to St. Peter will not fail even against all the combined powers of hell. The wise man will build his family life on the unchanging teachings of St. Peter and his successors. During the decades to come these families will be a beacon of hope to other families about to perish in the storm.

Fathers, you are central in God's plan for the revival of the family, the renewal of the Church, and the restoration of our culture. In the name of Jesus Christ our Lord, rise to the challenge and build your home on the Rock.

On the Shoulders of Giants:
A Tribute to My Father

James Burnham

If I have any weaknesses as a father, I have only myself to blame. In this age of victims, dysfunctional families, and easy alibis, I simply have no excuse. God blessed me with wonderful role models in my father and mother. Their lives are an enduring testimony of faithfulness to God and family. So if I have any strengths as a father, it is only because I stand on the shoulders of giants.

We buried my father, David Burnham, thirteen months ago. Just why God allowed him to die at the age of fifty-three, when six of his ten children still lived at home, the youngest only eleven years old, is a mystery to me. Sometimes I am tempted to shake my fist at God, and ask in Job-like indignation, "Why, Lord? Why would you, a loving Father, take my loving father from the family that needs him so desperately?" But in the midst of my grief and in those moments of not-so-quiet desperation, I find some consolation and strength in the heritage he left behind.

Admittedly, that consolation can be very small. What I *want* is his larger-than-life presence and his seemingly inexhaustible wisdom. I want him to tell me how to handle my two-year-old's tantrums, and how to protect my children from the seductions of our age. What I *have* is a handful of memories and the poor copy of his legacy that I reflect in my own character. But these deposits still hold his examples and convictions—and these are enough, with God's grace, to guide me in my own fathering.

David Burnham was a man of surpassing faithfulness to his Church, his family, and his principles. As a husband and father he understood that he was the domestic priest who had a fundamental obligation to help every member of his family become a saint. He made the words of Joshua his own: "As for me and my house, we will serve the LORD" (Joshua 24:15).

As priest of the home, Dad exercised a vigilant watch over our spiritual development. He insisted that we receive the sacraments frequently, and that we learn to really love and live our faith. He promoted daily prayer, and led the family Rosary. Every morning on the way to Mass, he would give us a mini-sermon on the essential doctrines of our faith. Sometimes after dinner, he would read from the Bible or a favorite spiritual book.

Dad loved and respected the Catholic Church. He would tolerate no criticism of priests, pointing out that only they could bring our Lord to us in the Holy Eucharist. Whenever possible, he took the whole family to daily Mass, and often told us, "Any career that doesn't allow time for daily Mass, isn't much of a career." He stressed that just "going through the motions" of prayer, Mass, and other sacraments was no guarantee of sanctity. "Rubbing shoulders with Christ won't help unless he rubs off on you," he would say, "for Judas spent three years with Christ, and yet Judas was probably lost."

My father put his family second only to God. Early in his marriage, Dad set a goal to have a business that would support him without consuming him. For the last twelve years of his life, he ran a successful real estate company from his office at home, amid constant interruptions from the younger children, who were being homeschooled. Never too busy to give advice, never too tired to discipline, he poured out his life in service to his family.

Dad often told us that he loved us, but he *always* did so after he disciplined us. He only spanked for two offenses: disobedience or a bad attitude. Being both willful and temperamental, I was notorious for receiving the lion's share of spankings! But I received a lion's share of affirmation as well.

Dad taught us to communicate honestly, and to apologize promptly. He was always willing to listen—even in an argument—and if he was wrong, he would quickly and sincerely ask for our forgiveness.

My father was generous with his time, money, and wisdom. He made time to counsel family and friends. He tithed to acknowledge the Lordship of Christ over his finances, and encouraged his children to do the same. He taught us to work when we were very young, to save money, and to be responsible for our own luxuries.

My father was a chaste man in a sex-soaked society. He was pure in speech and pure in mind. I never knew him to tell an off-color joke, or look lustfully at another woman. He taught his children modesty and chastity through the fidelity and respect he showed to Peggy, his wife of twenty-seven years.

Dad was thrilled to be alive. "Every day above ground is a good day," he'd quote from some otherwise forgettable movie. He loved being out in God's creation: farming, fishing, flying, trail-riding, scuba-diving, and subdividing. He taught us that God's creation can be enjoyed fully if it is used in his service.

My father was full of joy. His greatest charm was that he truly loved people. He made friends everywhere because of his winning smile and genuine emotions. He had a joke or a story for every occasion; some of his favorites he told again and again (and again!) until they became family proverbs.

My father was the most courageous man I ever knew. Friends and enemies alike regarded him as a man of integrity and principle. Dad had the courage of his convictions. He fought tirelessly for the causes he knew were right, no matter what the consequences. As a member of the local school board, he was often out-voted four to one as he fought against sex education, funding for faculty abortions, and the typical liberal agenda. On the Feast of the Holy Innocents, he took his family to stand in front of the Planned Parenthood clinic to protest the slaughter of innocent unborn children. For many years he presented "pro-life" classes for the seniors at the local high school. Shortly before he died, he erected a billboard that still declares to 25,000 passing cars every day: "Adoption, Not Abortion."

Even during his battle with cancer, Dad's faith never faltered. While he hated the thought of dying, he did not grow angry with God. He fought death with every ounce of his strength, but his war-cry was: "If God wants me to go, nothing can keep me; if God wants me to stay, nothing can take me." Dad told us the Tuesday before he died, that this was his Holy Week, that he was going "home," and that we should pray for the strength to go on after he was gone. It reminded me of Christ's words to the weeping women of Jerusalem, consoling them in the midst of his own terrible agony.

While we children still lived at home, Dad would bless and kiss each of us good night. As we got older, this simple ritual became an increasingly precious way of saying "I love you." Before I left Dad that last day at the hospital, I leaned over his bed to kiss him goodbye. He weakly raised his hand and blessed me for the last time. I couldn't stop the tears—he was a father and a family priest to the very end.

We brought him home the afternoon before he died. He had received all his sacraments and the Apostolic blessing. That night we gathered around him and read his favorite poems. Dad died peacefully as we read from the Psalms of King David.

Although the cancer ravaged his body, it purified his soul and confirmed his faith. As his strength failed, his eyes grew ever more luminous. Dad had often said, "The only mistake you can make in life is not to die a saint." Considering the way he lived and the way he died, I trust, by the grace of God, that he did not make that mistake.

When I wallow in self-pity, asking why I only had twenty-six years with my father, I have to stop and remember that at least I *had* twenty-six wonderful years with my dad. My younger brothers and sisters received much less. I know that many children didn't have good role models; many children grew up without any father at all. How can this tribute to my father apply to them?

I'm a cradle-Catholic father who was given every ingredient to become a good father. What about those fathers who didn't even have a recipe?

To answer this heartfelt concern, I should mention that David Burnham's own father was a non-practicing Mormon who often worked away from home from the time my dad was six. He died when Dad was only twelve. Although he didn't have many years with his dad, my father managed to leave an enduring legacy for his children. He made up, in one generation, all that had been lacking in his own upbringing. I am capable of *undoing*, in one generation, all that has been entrusted to me. One generation is all it takes; one generation is all we have.

As fathers, we have an obligation to give even more than we received. Let us father our families in such a way that when we die, our children will be able to stand on our shoulders and say: "I had such a wonderful father that if I have any weaknesses as a parent, I have only myself to blame."

December, 1994

What Scripture Teaches About Divorce and Remarriage

> "Between the baptized, 'a ratified and consummated marriage cannot be dissolved by any human power or for any reason other than death.'"
> —*Catechism of the Catholic Church*[1]

Jesus Teaches the Indissolubility of Marriage

The Gospels record Jesus' teaching on the indissolubility of marriage: to divorce from a valid marriage and remarry is to commit adultery.

> *"For this reason a man shall leave his father and mother and be joined to his wife, and the two shall become one flesh.' So they are no longer two but one flesh. What therefore God has joined together, let not man put asunder." And in the house the disciples asked him again about this matter. And he said to them, "Whoever divorces his wife and marries another, commits adultery against her; and if she divorces her husband and marries another, she commits adultery"* (Mark 10:7-12).

> *"Every one who divorces his wife and marries another commits adultery, and he who marries a woman divorced from her husband commits adultery"* (Luke 16:18).

St. Paul Teaches the Indissolubility of Marriage

St. Paul reverberates Jesus' teaching in Romans and 1st Corinthians.

Thus a married woman is bound by law to her husband as long as he lives; but if her husband dies she is discharged from the law concerning the husband. Accordingly, she will be called an adulteress if she lives with another man while her husband is alive. But if her husband dies she is free from that law, and if she marries another man she is not an adulteress (Romans 7:2-3).

The Greek verb for "she will be called" means "to bear the name, or title of." The verb indicates an ongoing sense in bearing the title of adulteress. For a person to unlawfully remarry constitutes not just a one-time *act* of adultery, but a continuing *state* of adultery. As the *Catechism of the Catholic Church* declares, "the remarried spouse is then in a situation of public and permanent adultery."[2] The reason a remarriage before the death of one's spouse is adulterous is that the first marriage bond still exists. Until death separates spouses, the marriage covenant is in full force.

To the married I give charge, not I but the LORD, that the wife should not separate from her husband (but if she does, let her remain single or else be reconciled to her husband)—and that the husband should not divorce his wife.... A wife is bound to her husband as long as he lives. If the husband dies, she is free to be married to whom she wishes, only in the LORD (1 Corinthians 7:10-11, 39).

In addition to being very challenging, these Scripture passages from Mark, Luke, Romans, and 1st Corinthians are also very clear. Remarriage after a divorce from a valid marriage (with the first spouse still living) is adultery. Those who want to justify remarriage seldom start with these scriptures. Instead they usually begin with Deuteronomy 24 and then move to the "exception clauses" in Matthew 5 and 19.

A Temporary Provision for "Hard Hearts"

Doesn't Moses permit divorce in Deuteronomy 24?

"When a man takes a wife and marries her, if then she finds no favor in his eyes because he has found some indecency in her, and he writes her a bill of divorce and puts it in her hand and sends her out of his house, and she departs out of his house, and if she goes and becomes another man's wife, and the latter husband dislikes her and writes her a bill of divorce and puts it in her hand and sends her out of his house, or if the latter husband

dies, who took her to be his wife, then her former husband, who sent her away, may not take her again to be his wife, after she has been defiled; for that is an abomination before the LORD...." (Deuteronomy 24:1-4).

Before examining Deuteronomy 24, we must keep in mind that many parts of the Mosaic Law were either rendered obsolete or perfected by the New Covenant. According to the *Catechism of the Catholic Church* (section 1984), "The Law of the Gospel fulfills and surpasses the Old Law and brings it to perfection ... by reforming the heart, the root of human acts." Therefore, many of the Mosaic laws were provisional, designed to restrain sin until the coming of Christ.

Deuteronomy 24:1-4 is a provisional regulation against unlimited divorce where a woman could be divorced again and again by the same husband. This was extremely degrading to wives. Moses is not encouraging divorce, but through this legislation he is regulating and restraining runaway divorce practices.

Jesus clearly tells us that Moses allowed divorce only because of "hardness of heart" (Matthew 19:7-9). The abundant graces available in the New Covenant will transform our selfish hearts of stone (Jeremiah 31 and Ezekiel 36) and enable us to love one spouse until death. Jesus perfects the intent of the law's restraint by restoring the indissolubility of marriage.

The New Covenant often perfects the law's restraint. One clear example is the legislation concerning revenge. Moses' law sought to restrain unlimited revenge by restricting retaliation to "an eye for an eye and a tooth for a tooth" (Exodus 21:24). Christ goes beyond restraining revenge and establishes a higher standard that prohibits revenge altogether (Matthew 5:38-39). Likewise, Christ goes beyond restraining divorce and reestablishes God's original plan of indissolubility (Matthew 19:3-9).

It is instructive to note which scriptures a person uses to build his position on divorce and remarriage. Jesus goes to Genesis and the Creator's original intention for marriage, while the Pharisees appeal to Moses' provisional divorce legislation for hard hearts. It is odd that some Christians use Deuteronomy to argue for divorce and remarriage. This is the same scripture the Pharisees misused in an attempt to entrap Jesus.

And Pharisees came up to him and tested him by asking, "Is it lawful to divorce one's wife for any cause?" He answered, "Have you not read that he who made them from the beginning made them male and female, and said, 'For this reason a man shall leave his father and mother and be joined to his wife, and the two shall become one flesh'? So they are no longer two but one flesh. What therefore God has joined together, let not man put asunder." They said to him, "Why then did Moses command one to give a certificate of divorce, and to put her away?" He said to them, "For your hardness of heart Moses allowed you to divorce your wives, but from the beginning it was not so. And I say to you: whoever divorces his wife, except for unchastity, and marries another, commits adultery" (Matthew 19:3-9).

Christians are people who are regenerated (that is, born again) with new hearts energized by the Holy Spirit. A "hardhearted Christian" is a contradiction in terms. The abundant graces in the New Covenant make it possible for spouses to fulfill the creator's original intention for lifelong marriages. Moses' legislation for hard hearts has been supplanted by the higher New Covenant standard of indissoluble sacramental marriages.[3]

The "Exception Clauses" in Matthew 5 and 19

Yes, but doesn't Jesus make exceptions to his teachings on indissolubility in St. Matthew?

"It was also said, 'Whoever divorces his wife, let him give her a certificate of divorce.' But I say to you that every one who divorces his wife, except on the ground of unchastity [porneia], *makes her an adulteress* [moicheuo]; *and whoever marries a divorced woman commits adultery* [moicheuo]" (Matthew 5:31-32).

"And I say to you: whoever divorces his wife, except for unchastity [porneia], *and marries another, commits adultery* [moicheuo]" (Matthew 19:9).

Many English translations of Matthew 5:32 and 19:9 imply that the exception is for sexual immorality. These translations give the impression that adultery and other types of unchastity dissolve the marriage bond and thus are exceptions to Jesus' teaching on indissolubility.[4]

The Greek word for adultery (*moicheia*-noun, *moicheuo*-verb) is used twice in Matthew 5:32 and once in 19:9, to describe the sin of remarriage. But adultery is not the word used as the *grounds* for divorce. Rather, the Greek word *porneia*, loosely translated as "unchastity" in the RSV, is the basis for the exception. In scripture, the word *porneia* can be used in a wide sense to include any type of sexual immorality. It can also be used in a narrow sense to denote a particular type of sexual sin, namely incestuous "marriage" among close relatives. Matthew 5:32 and 19:9 can be shown to be using *porneia* in this narrow sense of unlawful marriages.

The Council of Jerusalem in Acts 15 met to deal with the question of the binding nature of the Mosaic laws upon the Gentiles converting to Christianity. The Apostle James expressed the decision of the Council not to make the ceremonial laws binding for Gentile converts, except for four requirements:

> *"Therefore my judgment is that we should not trouble those of the Gentiles who turn to God, but should write to them to abstain from the pollutions of idols and from unchastity* [porneia] *and from what is strangled and from blood"* (Acts 15:19-20).

All four exceptions come from Leviticus.[5] Therefore, to interpret the meaning of *porneia* in Acts 15, we should draw upon the context provided by Leviticus 17 and 18, which condemns incestuous unions and marriages among close relatives. These incestuous "marriages" were universally forbidden to the Jews (Leviticus 18:6-18) as well as to the Gentiles from the time of Noah.[6] Therefore, *porneia* in Acts 15 is used specifically to forbid incestuous "marriages."

In 1st Corinthians, St. Paul also uses this specific sense of *porneia* when he condemns an incestuous relationship between a man and his father's wife.

> *It is actually reported that there is immorality* [porneia] *among you, and of a kind that is not found even among pagans; for a man is living with his father's wife* (1 Corinthians 5:1).

Therefore, in Matthew 5:32 and 19:9, Jesus is not making adultery an exception to the indissolubility of a valid marriage. His exception for *porneia* refers to those converts who find themselves in unlawful marriages. These illicit unions are not bound by the law of indissolubility because they were not valid marriages in the first place.

Although not a literal translation, the accurate meaning of Matthew 5:32 is captured by the translation in the *New American Bible*:

> *"But I say to you, whoever divorces his wife (unless the marriage is unlawful) causes her to commit adultery, and whoever marries a divorced woman commits adultery."*

There is a simple way for readers who find all these Greek terms confusing to quickly grasp the proper meaning of Matthew 5:32 and 19:9. Ask yourself, "How did the Greek-speaking early Church Fathers understand this passage?" After all, Greek was their mother tongue and any nuances in these exception clauses would be best understood by a Greek-speaking Church Father.

You will not find a single Greek-speaking early Church Father agreeing with the modern Protestant interpretations of Matthew 5 and 19 and granting exceptions to Christ's law of indissolubility.

In addition, there is only one Latin-speaking early Church Father, Ambrosiaster, who allowed remarriage after divorce. In describing his commentaries, *The Catholic Encyclopedia* (1913) says: "Reference to the Greek text is rarely found: in fact the writer seems to be ignorant of the Greek language."[7] Every other Latin-speaking early Church Father and Church Council taught indissolubility. The unanimous voice of the early Church is that marriage is indissoluble and that divorce from a legitimate marriage cannot be followed by remarriage.[8] This early Church teaching on indissolubility was undisputed in the west until the sixteenth century. Thereafter, the dissoluble view of marriage proliferated throughout the world, especially western culture, along with Protestantism.

The *Catechism of the Catholic Church*

Today there are numerous Catholics in many countries who have recourse to civil divorce and contract new unions. In fidelity to the words of Jesus Christ—"Whoever divorces his wife and marries another, commits adultery against her; and if she divorces her husband and marries another, she commits adultery" [Mark 10:11-12]—the Church maintains that a new union cannot be recognized as valid, if the first marriage was. If the divorced are remarried civilly, they find themselves in a situation that objectively contravenes God's law (section 1650).

Persons who find themselves in such invalid unions should consult section 84 of *The Role of the Christian Family in the Modern World* and sections 1650 and 1651 of the *Catechism of the Catholic Church* for the Church's directives on how to remedy these situations.

Divorced Men Can Bear Witness to Covenant Keeping

I extend a special plea for divorced men to bear witness to the indissolubility of marriage. Some men have rejected St. Joseph's Covenant Keepers because our emphasis on indissolubility has been painful to hear. Remember that there will *always* be pain associated with marital breakup. If divorced men choose the path of denial and avoidance, then the pain gets passed on to subsequent generations. Our silence insures that the hurt increases at an intensifying rate and penetrates into future generations with greater and greater ease.

Divorced men who honestly face the pain of their marital dissolution and find forgiveness in Christ for their personal failures can often be effective witnesses to the indissolubility of marriage. Through the pain of their witness they can encourage others to save their marriages. Such witnesses are also critical for the next generation as they prepare for marriage.

Why Is This Truth Missed by Sincere Protestants?

In 1517, Martin Luther formally broke covenant with the One, Holy, Catholic, and Apostolic Church. The Catholic Church did have problems in need of correction and renewal at the time of Luther's break. Yet serious ecclesiastical problems, just like serious marital problems, don't justify a "divorce."

Only three years after he severed ties with Rome, Luther wrote the *Babylonian Captivity* (1520) in which he denied the sacramentality of marriage and declared that marriage should be under civil jurisdiction instead of ecclesiastical. Indissolubility disappeared under the theory that marriage is merely a civil contract. These views launched the modern secularization of marriage and explosion of divorce.

How could Luther make such a profound mistake about marriage? Why has *every* major branch of Christendom that has broken off from the Catholic Church embraced exceptions to Christ's teaching on indissolubility?

Beliefs about marriage are interrelated with beliefs about the Church. History shows that when any group breaks covenant with the One, Holy, Catholic, and Apostolic Church it is just a matter of time until it allows the breaking of the marriage covenant. In Luther's case it took just three years. Ecclesiology (beliefs about the Church) will inevitably influence one's beliefs about marriage. Genuine renewal of marriage and family life will require reexamining the big questions about the Church.

Endnotes

Foreword by Archbishop J. Francis Stafford

[1] David Blankenhorn, *Fatherless America* (New York: Basic Books, 1995), p. 1.

[2] Blankenhorn, *Fatherless America*, p. 2.

[3] David Popenoe, *Life Without Father* (New York: The Free Press, 1996), p. 20.

[4] Paternal death does not have the same adverse effects on children as paternal abandonment. See *Fatherless America,* pp. 22-23, and *Life Without Father*, pp. 151-152.

[5] "Family Values Gain Control," *The Wall Street Journal*, December 12, 1995, p. A6.

[6] Smith & Jarjoura, "Social Structure and Crime Victimization," *Journal of Research in Crime and Delinquency* 25, no. 1 (February, 1988), pp. 27-52.

[7] Lawrence Kubie, "The Desire to Become Both Sexes," *Psychoanalytic Quarterly* 43, no. 3 (July 1974), p. 370.

[8] U.S. Bureau of the Census, "Poverty in the United States: 1992," p. xvi.

[9] U.S. Bureau of the Census, *Current Population Reports*, cited in *The Index of Leading Cultural Indicators* by William J. Bennett.

[10] *The Role of the Christian Family in the Modern World [Familiaris Consortio]*, section 25.

Chapter 1 — The Heart of Fatherhood

[1] In the *New American Bible [NAB]*, Malachi does not have a chapter 4. This same verse is found in the *NAB* as Malachi 3:24.

[2] *The Role of the Christian Family in the Modern World [Familiaris Consortio]*, section 25.

[3] *The Role of the Christian Family in the Modern World*, section 25.

[4] *Catechism of the Catholic Church* (Ligouri, Missouri: Ligouri Publications, 1994), section 176.

Chapter 2 — An Evangelical Discovers Covenant Keeping

[1] *The Role of the Christian Family in the Modern World [Familiaris Consortio]*, section 20.

[2] See Appendix 2: "What Scripture Teaches About Divorce and Remarriage."

[3] "I earnestly call upon pastors and the whole community of the faithful to help the divorced, and with solicitous care to make sure that they do not consider themselves as separated from the Church, for as baptized persons they can, and indeed must, share in her life. They should be encouraged to listen to the word of God, to attend the Sacrifice of the Mass, to persevere in prayer, to contribute to works of charity and to community efforts in favor of justice, to bring up their children in the Christian faith, to cultivate the spirit and practice of penance and thus implore, day by day, God's grace. Let the Church pray for them, encourage them and show herself a merciful mother, and thus sustain them in faith and hope.

"However, the Church reaffirms her practice, which is based upon Sacred Scripture, of not admitting to Eucharistic Communion divorced persons who have remarried. They are unable to be admitted thereto from the fact that their state and condition of life objectively contradict that union of love between Christ and the Church which is signified and effected by the Eucharist. Besides this, there is another special pastoral reason: if these people were admitted to the Eucharist, the faithful would be led into error and confusion regarding the Church's teaching regarding the indissolubility of marriage.

"Reconciliation in the sacrament of Penance, which would open the way to the Eucharist, can only be granted to those who, repenting of having broken the sign of the Covenant and of fidelity to Christ, are sincerely ready to undertake a way of life that is no longer in contradiction to the indissolubility of marriage. This means, in practice, that when, for serious reasons, such as for example the children's upbringing, a man and a woman cannot satisfy the obligation to separate, they 'take on themselves the duty to live in complete continence, that is, by abstinence from the acts proper to married couples.'

"By acting in this way, the Church professes her own fidelity to Christ and to His truth. At the same time she shows motherly concern for these children of hers, especially those who, through no fault of their own, have been abandoned by their legitimate partner" (*The Role of the Christian Family in the Modern World* [*Familiaris Consortio*], section 84). This teaching is repeated in the *Catechism of the Catholic Church,* sections 1650 and 1651.

[4] The following books are invaluable for discovering what the Catholic Church really teaches and why:

- (1) *The Catechism of the Catholic Church* (Ligouri, Missouri: Ligouri Publications, 1994).
- (2) Mark P. Shea, *This Is My Body: An Evangelical Discovers the Real Presence* (Front Royal, Virginia: Christendom Press, 1993).
- (3) Mark P. Shea, *By What Authority: An Evangelical Discovers Catholic Tradition* (Huntington, Indiana: Our Sunday Visitor, 1996).

- (4) William A. Jurgens, *The Faith of the Early Fathers*, 3 Vols. (Collegeville, Minnesota: Liturgical Press, 1970).
- (5) Jim Burnham and Fr. Frank Chacon, *Beginning Apologetics I: How to Explain and Defend the Catholic Faith* (Farmington, New Mexico: San Juan Catholic Seminars [P. O. Box 5253, Farmington, New Mexico 87499-5253], 1996).
- (6) David B. Currie, *Born Fundamentalist, Born Again Catholic* (San Francisco: Ignatius Press, 1996).
- (7) Patrick Madrid, editor, *Surprised by Truth: Eleven Converts Give the Biblical and Historical Reasons for Becoming Catholic* (San Diego: Basilica Press, 1994). Portions of this chapter are adapted from *Surprised By Truth*, pp. 77-100.
- (8) John Henry Newman, *Mary, the Second Eve* (Rockford, Illinois: TAN Books, 1982).
- (9) Leslie Rumble and Charles M. Carty, *Radio Replies*, 3 Vols. (Rockford, Illinois: TAN Books, 1979).
- (10) *The Navarre Bible*, 12 Volumes on the New Testament (Princeton, New Jersey: Scepter, 1988-1993).
- (11) Henry G. Graham, *Where We Got the Bible: Our Debt to the Catholic Church* (San Diego: Catholic Answers, 1997).
- (12) James Cardinal Gibbons, *The Faith of Our Fathers* (Rockford, Illinois: TAN Books, 1980).
- (13) John Henry Newman, *An Essay on the Development of Christian Doctrine* (Notre Dame, Indiana: University of Notre Dame, 1989).
- (14) Scott Butler, Norman Dahlgren, and David Hess, *Jesus, Peter, and the Keys* (Santa Barbara, California: Queenship Publishing, 1996).
- (15) Ludwig Ott, *Fundamentals of Catholic Dogma* (Rockford, Illinois: TAN Books, 1974).

[5] *The Role of the Christian Family in the Modern World* [*Familiaris Consortio*], section 75.

[6] Some people question the Catholic practice of calling priests "father," citing Matthew 23:9, where Jesus says "call no man father." In Matthew 23:1-12, when Jesus tells us to call no man "father" or "teacher," he is using hyperbole to stress that all legitimate authority and truth come ultimately from God. But we know this is not an absolute prohibition, because the Scriptures repeatedly call men "father" and "teacher" without contradicting Jesus' teaching in Matthew 23. In Acts 7:2 and 22:1, St. Stephen and St. Paul call the Jewish religious leaders "fathers." St. Paul calls the Corinthians "my beloved children.... For I became your father in Christ Jesus through the gospel" (1 Corinthians 4:14-15). St. Paul says he treated the Thessalonians "like a father with his children" (1 Thessalonians 2:11). Also see 1 Timothy 1:2 and Titus 1:4, where St. Paul calls Timothy and Titus his true children in the faith. Catholics rightly call their priests "father" because of their service in the household of faith (1 Timothy 3:15).

Chapter 3 — Affirming Christ's Lordship Over Our Families

[1] Robert W. Fogel, *Wall Street Journal*, January 9, 1996.

[2] *The Role of the Christian Family in the Modern World*, section 75.

[3] *On the Kingship of Christ* [*Quas Primas*], December 11, 1925. Although this encyclical has been available for over seventy years, I find that fewer than one in twenty Catholics have ever heard of it and fewer still have read it. This encyclical summarizes both the Old Testament and the New Testament teaching on the kingship of Christ. The summary concludes by saying, "It was surely right, then, in view of the common teaching of the sacred books, that the Catholic Church ... is the kingdom of Christ on earth." How many modern Catholics realize that Christ is not only king during this age, but that the Catholic Church is the visible expression of his kingdom? This encyclical is available, for free, from EWTN's website, www.ewtn.com.

[4] *On the Kingship of Christ.*

[5] John W. Miller, *Biblical Faith and Fathering* (Mahwah, New Jersey: Paulist Press, 1989), p. 13.

[6] *On Devotion to the Sacred Heart* [*Haurietis Aquas*], 1956. Available on the Internet from www.ewtn.com.

[7] Preface, *Mass of the Sacred Heart.*

[8] *On Devotion to the Sacred Heart.*

[9] *On Devotion to the Sacred Heart.*

[10] We realize that the enthronement of the Sacred Heart may be unfamiliar to our Protestant readers. We strongly encourage our Protestant brothers to investigate this biblical and historical way to acknowledge Christ's kingship over your family. Contact the Family Life Center for a list of resources on devotion to the Sacred Heart.

[11] Any day of the year is a good time for an enthronement of the Sacred Heart in your home. Some other appropriate feast days are: Feast of the Holy Family (after Christmas), Feast of the Divine Mercy (Sunday after Easter), and Ascension Thursday (forty days after Easter).

Chapter 4 — Following St. Joseph, the Loving Leader and Head of the Holy Family

[1] Pius XI's 1930 encyclical *Christian Marriage* [*Casti Connubii*], p. 15 of the Daughters of St. Paul edition.

[2] Clayton C. Barbeau, *The Father of the Family* (Huntington, Indiana: Our Sunday Visitor, 1990), pp. 8-9.

[3] *The Catholic World Report*, October 1994, p. 9.

[4] The Greek word used in the New Testament to describe headship is *kephale*. See *Recovering Biblical Manhood & Womanhood: A Response to Evangelical Feminism*, edited by John Piper and Wayne Grudem, Appendix 1, "The Meaning of Kephale ('Head'): A Response to Recent Studies" (Wheaton, Illinois: Crossway Books, 1991), pp. 424-468.

[5] "Human love finds in Trinitarian love a model of perfect loving and giving" (*L'Osservatore Romano*, January 22, 1997, citing John Paul II's address on December 7, 1996).

[6] 1880 encyclical *Arcanum divinae sapientae,The Great Encyclical Letters of Pope Leo XIII* (Rockford, Illinois: TAN Books, 1995), pp. 64–65.

[7] Pope Benedict XV, *Motu Proprio* (1920); Pope Pius XI, *Divini Redemptoris* (1937); Pope Leo XIII, *Arcanum*, (1880).

Pope Pius XII's 1930 encyclical *Christian Marriage* [*Casti Connubii*] reaffirmed the continuing relevance of Pope Leo XIII's encyclical *Arcanum* which taught the headship of St. Joseph, the headship of the husband, and the equality of husbands and wives within the Christian family. "We follow the footsteps of Our Predecessor, Leo XIII, of happy memory, whose Encyclical *Arcanum*, published fifty years ago [from 1930], We hereby confirm and make Our own, and while We wish to expound more fully certain points called for by the circumstances of our times, nevertheless We declare that, **far from being obsolete, it retains its full force at the present day**." These encyclicals are available at EWTN's website, www.ewtn.com.

[8] *Letter to Families*, section 23.

[9] *Christian Marriage*, pp. 15-16 in the Daughters of St. Paul edition.

[10] *Christian Marriage*, p. 16.

[11] Thomas Howard, *C.S. Lewis Man of Letters* (San Francisco: Ignatius Press, 1987), p. 25.

[12] David Blankenhorn, *Fatherless America* (New York: Basic Books, 1995); Maggie Gallagher, *The Abolition of Marriage* (Washington, D.C: Regnery Publishing, 1996); David Popenoe, *Life Without Father* (New York: The Free Press, 1996).

[13] Recommended reading on the complementarian view of role relations:
- St. John Chrysostom, Homily XX on Ephesians 5:22-23, Philip Schaff, editor, *The Nicene and Post-Nicene Fathers* (Grand Rapids, Michigan: Eerdmans, 1980), Vol. XIII, pp.143-152.
- St. Augustine, Sermon 51.
- St. Thomas Aquinas, *Commentary on St. Paul's Epistle to the Ephesians*, translated by Matthew L. Lamb (Albany, New York: Magi Books, 1966), pp. 216-226.
- Pope Leo XIII's 1878 encyclical *Socialism, Communism, Nihilism* [*Quod Apostolici Muneris*] (Rockford, Illinois: TAN Books, 1995), pp. 28-30.
- Pope Leo XIII's 1880 encyclical *Christian Marriage* [*Arcarnum divinae sapientiae*] (Rockford, Illinois: TAN Books, 1995), pp. 64-67.
- Pope Pius XI's 1930 encyclical *Christian Marriage* [*Casti Connubii*], pp. 15-16 in the Daughters of St. Paul edition.
- James F. Murray, Jr. and Bianca M. Murray, translators *Dear Newly-weds: Pope Pius XII Speaks to Young Couples* (New York: Farrar, Straus, and Cudahy, 1961).

- Stephen Clark, *Man and Woman in Christ: An Examination of the Roles of Men and Women in Light of Scripture and the Social Sciences* (Ann Arbor, Michigan: Servant Books, 1980).
- John Piper and Wayne Grudem, editors, *Recovering Biblical Manhood & Womanhood: A Response to Evangelical Feminism* (Wheaton, Illinois: Crossway Books, 1991). See especially chapter 10, pages 198-200 and the corresponding notes on pages 499-503. This entire book is available on-line at www.cbmw.org.

Today there is considerable divergence of opinion on the interpretation of Ephesians 5:21 which says, "Be subject to one another out of reverence for Christ." Does this verse teach mutual submission as many people claim?

Ephesians 5:21 is clearly a summary verse for what follows through the end of chapter five and into chapter six. Many assume from a casual reading of the English text that Ephesians 5:21 is describing what has been popularly called "mutual submission" of husbands and wives. There are three reasons why the text does not support this interpretation.

The first reason is the immediate context of the passage. Any text, that is a verse of scripture, can become a pretext if it is taken out of context. Ephesians 5:21 can't be speaking of "mutual submission," because Ephesians 5:22-33 only speaks to wives about submission. Husbands are commanded to love their wives in a Christlike fashion, but they are not told to submit to their wives.

The second reason is the wider context of the passage. Everyone agrees that Ephesians 5:21 is a summary verse for the passage that runs from Ephesians 5:21 all the way to 6:9. If 5:21 is commanding "mutual submission," then St. Paul is advocating mutual submission not only of spouses but also of parents and children. Any thinking parent instantly recognizes that the notion of mutual submission between parents and children is absurd.

The third reason is that modern linguistic research in first-century Greek literature reveals that the word *hupotasso* (submit to, be subject to) always implies submission to an authority and was never understood to mean mutual submission.

Below are examples from the research from New Testament scholar Wayne Grudem's book, *Recovering Biblical Manhood and Womanhood* (199-200), showing how the word *hupotasso* is consistently used in the New Testament:

> Luke 2:51 - submission of Jesus to the authority of his parents
> Luke 10:17 - demons being subject to the disciples
> Romans 13:1, Titus 3:1, 1 Peter 2:13 - citizens being subject to governing authorities

1 Corinthians 15:27, Ephesians 1:22 - the universe being subject
to Christ

1 Corinthians 15:28 - Christ being subject to God the Father

1 Corinthians 16:15-16 - Church members being subject to
Church leaders

Hebrews 12:9, James 4:7 - Christians being subject to God

Ephesians 5:24 - the Church being subject to Christ

Colossians 3:18, Titus 2:5, 1 Peter 3:5 - wives being subject to
their husbands

Notice that none of these roles are ever reversed: husbands are never told to be submissive to their wives, nor government to citizens, nor disciples to demons, and so on. The phrase "submit to one another" in Ephesians 5:21 is a summary verse talking about wives submitting to husbands, children to parents, and servants to masters (6:4-8).

Some have interpreted John Paul II's remarks in *Mulieris Dignitatem* to be advocating the mutual submission of spouses in a manner that contradicts the tradition of the Church. In this apostolic letter, which the Holy Father has called a biblical-theological meditation on the dignity of women, he emphasizes the mutual respect and love spouses must have for each other. However, we must always assume that the Pope is teaching within the tradition of his predecessors.

[14] Rev. Paul J. Gorman, *Life with Joseph* (St. Paul, Minnesota: Leaflet Missal Company, 1988), p. 73.

[15] Any doubters are encouraged to read David Blankenhorn's *Fatherless America* and Barbara Dafoe Whitehead's *The Divorce Culture* (New York: Alfred A. Knopf, 1997).

[16] Pope Leo XIII's 1889 encyclical *On Devotion to St. Joseph* [*Quamquam Pluries*]. This excellent encyclical can be downloaded from www.ewtn.com.

[17] John Paul II's 1989 apostolic exhortation *Guardian of the Redeemer*, section 20.

[18] *Guardian of the Redeemer*, section 12.

[19] "Now the divine house which Joseph ruled with the authority of a father, contained within its limits the scarce-born Church. From the same fact that the most holy Virgin is the mother of Jesus Christ is she the mother of all Christians whom she bore on Mount Calvary amid the supreme throes of the Redemption; Jesus Christ is, in a manner, the first-born of Christians, who by the adoption and redemption are his brothers. And for such reasons the Blessed Patriarch looks upon the multitude of Christians who make up the Church as confided specially to his trust—this limitless family spread over the earth, over which, because he is the spouse of Mary and the Father of Jesus Christ he holds, as it were, a paternal authority. It is natural and worthy that as the Blessed Joseph ministered to all the needs of the family at Nazareth and girt it about with his protection, he should now cover

with the cloak of his heavenly patronage and defend the Church of Jesus Christ" (*On Devotion to St. Joseph*, section 3).

[20] Francis L. Filas, *Joseph and Jesus: A Theological Study of Their Relationship* (Milwaukee, Wisconsin: Bruce Publishing Company, 1952), quoting Bossuet, an eighteenth-century writer, p. 104.

Chapter 5 — Loving Our Wives All Our Lives

[1] *Catechism of the Catholic Church*, sections 1963, 1964 and 1984.

[2] *Catechism of the Catholic Church*, sections 1613 and 1601. Notice that Catholic marriages are not the only sacramental marriages. Every valid marriage between baptized Christians is a sacrament, a source of God's life-giving grace. By Christ's design, *all* sacramental marriages have graces available for perfecting the couple's love and strengthening their indissoluble unity (*CCC*, section 1641). The more we appreciate this sacrament, the more we can appropriate its graces for our marriages.

[3] Section 57.

[4] See Matthew 6:12,14-15, 18:21-35; Ephesians 4:26, 30-32; Colossians 3:12-13; and Hebrews 12:14-15.

[5] John 20:21-23. The early Church Fathers clearly taught that the Apostolic power to forgive sins was passed on to their successors, the bishops and priests of the Catholic Church. See Jurgens, sections 493, 553, 602, 637, and 855.

[6] In his 1984 apostolic exhortation, *Reconciliation and Penance* [*Reconciliatio et Paenitentia*], Pope John Paul II repeats Pius XII's prophetic words, "the sin of the century is the loss of the sense of sin" (section 18).

[7] *The Role of the Christian Family in the Modern World* [*Familiaris Consortio*], section 21.

[8] This book is not intended to be an exhaustive treatment of these sacraments. For a full explanation of the sacraments see *Catechism of the Catholic Church*, sections 1066–1690.

[9] Ecclesiastes 4:12.

[10] Michael J. McManus, *Marriage Savers: Helping Your Friends and Family Stay Married* (Grand Rapids, Michigan: Zondervan, 1993), p. 105.

[11] *Marriage Savers*, p. 91.

[12] *Marriage Savers*, p. 92

[13] *Marriage Savers*, p. 91.

Chapter 6 — Turning Our Hearts Toward Our Children

[1] A Johnston Company synthesis of eighteen youth studies and values-oriented clients as listed in McDowell's Research Digest.

[2] Sociologist John Robinson of the University of Maryland, *USA Today*, May 10, 1991.

[3] George Barna, *Generation Next: What Every Parent and Youth Worker Needs to Know About the Attitudes and Beliefs of Today's Youth* (Glendale, California: Barna Research Group, 1995), pp. 36-43; Josh McDowell, *The Myth of Sex Education* (San Bernadino, California: Here's Life Publishers, 1990), pp. 38-39.

[4] According to one study, the average five-year-old spends only twenty-five minutes a week in close interaction with his father. In contrast, the same child spends twenty-five hours per week in close interaction with the TV. Josh McDowell, *The Myth of Sex Education* (San Bernadino, California: Here's Life Publishers, 1990), p. 46, citing *Focus on the Family Bulletin*, 1989.

[5] See David Blankenhorn's *Fatherless America* (New York: Basic Books, 1995), David Popenoe's *Life Without Father* (New York: The Free Press, 1996), Maggie Gallagher's *The Abolition of Marriage*, (Washington, D.C.: Regnery Publishing, 1996) and Barbara Dafoe Whitehead's *The Divorce Culture* (New York: Alfred A. Knopf, 1997).

[6] "The Jewish Family: Ancient Covenants, Modern Challenges," published in *The Family in America*, September 1995.

[7] Section 2186.

[8] Section 2195.

[9] *The Washington Times*, November 27, 1995, reporting on a survey published by *Who's Who Among American High School Students*.

[10] *USA Today*, September 11, 1996.

Chapter 7 — Educating Our Children in the Discipline and Instruction of the Lord

[1] *Hear, O sons, a father's instruction, and be attentive, that you may gain insight; for I give you good precepts: do not forsake my teaching. When I was a son with my father, tender, the only one in the sight of my mother, he taught me, and said to me, "Let your heart hold fast my words; keep my commandments, and live; do not forget, and do not turn away from the words of my mouth. Get wisdom; get insight"* (Proverbs 4:1-5).

[2] *New York Times* and CBS News poll, April 1993.

³ John Paul II's 1979 apostolic exhortation *Catechesis in Our Time*
[*Catechesi Tradendae*], section 68. Because of the invasive secularism
in our society, many parents are opting to go beyond home catechesis
and embrace homeschooling. To learn more about Catholic
homeschooling, contact the Family Life Center for a free list of materials.

⁴ George Barna, *The Future of the American Family* (Chicago, Illinois:
Moody Press, 1993), p. 101.

⁵ *The Role of the Christian Family in the Modern World*, section 25.

⁶ *Catechesis in Our Time*, section 68.

⁷ We recommend the *Faith and Life Series* published by Ignatius Press. It
is the best catechetical curriculum for children grades one to eight. It
also makes an excellent men's small group program. Let the men in
your group learn their faith from the actual texts they will be using
with their children. The teacher's manuals for each grade contain
background information, chalkboard illustrations, the main points to
convey with each lesson, and references for further study. So your
group will not need eight separate classes, cluster grades 1-3, 4-5, and
6-8 into three classes.

For men who don't have a small group to assist them, the Family Life
Center has produced a video cassette showing a father teaching his
children using the *Faith and Life Series.* Small groups should try to
have their own live demonstration. A taped or live demonstration will
ease men's fears and help convince them that teaching the faith is a
task the average father can easily accomplish. Do not underestimate
the need for anxiety-reducing demonstrations. These, coupled with a
first-hand look at the *Faith and Life* curriculum, will quadruple the
number of men who will actually catechize their children.

As a companion, or alternative, to the *Faith and Life Series,* use the new
Catechism of the Catholic Church. Every Catholic men's group should
have classes, cassettes, and books available to explain the new catechism. As men grow in their knowledge of the faith, they will feel
increasingly comfortable catechizing their children.

⁸ A generation ago Archbishop Fulton Sheen was telling parents: "The
best way I know to ensure that your children will lose their faith is to
send them to Catholic colleges." Fortunately, there are now some
excellent and faithful Catholic colleges in the United States.

⁹ I suggest that every parent who has children preparing for college take
the following practical steps:

• Make a commitment to protect your child's faith, no matter what the
cost or sacrifice. After all, what does it profit your child to gain the
whole world, if he loses his soul in the process? (See Matthew 16:26.)

• Contact the Family Life Center for a list of recommended Catholic
colleges.

- Request and carefully read catalogs from each institution you are considering.

- Visit as many campuses as you can, perhaps incorporating them into family vacations. Investigate such things as: dormitory rules on social visits from the opposite sex, the availability of traditional Catholic devotions such as the Rosary, the bookstore's textbooks for the various courses, and so on.

- Interview several teachers and ask whether the school is faithful to the Magisterium of the Church and provides solid spiritual formation. Obtain the names of several graduates. Call them to get a feel for what kind of person this program helps to form. Just as you wouldn't undergo major surgery without a second opinion, don't accept whatever a glossy brochure tells you about a college. Get some second opinions; do some investigating.

- Make a decision based on: (i) how this college will promote your child's faith; and (ii) how it will foster his academic development. Don't let your decision get sidetracked by sports programs and prestigious degrees. Remember that any sacrifice for an authentic Catholic education will pay eternal dividends in the lives of your children.

Chapter 8 — Protecting Our Families

[1] Title of John Paul II's 1989 encyclical on St. Joseph.

[2] *Changing and Becoming*, Grade 4, The New Creation Series (Dubuque, Iowa: Brown ROA Publishing, 1989), p. 12. We refrained from printing this quotation due to its explicit nature.

[3] Section 143. Contact the Daughters of St. Paul, or the Family Life Center, to obtain a copy of *The Truth and Meaning of Human Sexuality: Guidelines for Education within the Family*.

[4] This $30,000 ad was paid for by Catholics for a Free Choice, which is headed by Frances Kissling, a former abortion facility administrator and past executive director of the National Abortion Federation. See Donna Steichen, *Ungodly Rage: The Hidden Face of Catholic Feminism* (San Francisco: Ignatius Press, 1991), pp. 320-322. Ms. Cooney also served on the task force that wrote the sex education guidelines for the United States Catholic Conference (USCC).

[5] *Washington Star News*, May 3, 1973, cited in Randy Engel, *Sex Education: The Final Plague* (Rockford, Illinois: TAN Books, 1993), p. 4.

[6] *American Atheist*, March 1988, cited in *On Watch*, January 1991.

[7] Section 64.

[8] *Catechism of the Council of Trent* (1566): "In the explanation of this [Sixth] Commandment, however, the pastor has need of great caution and prudence, and should treat with great delicacy a subject which requires brevity rather than copiousness of exposition. For it is to be

feared that if he explained in too great detail or at length the ways in which this Commandment is violated, he might unintentionally speak of subjects which, instead of extinguishing, usually serve rather to inflame corrupt passion" (Rockford, Illinois: TAN Books, 1982), p. 431.

[9] Sections 2521 and 2522.

[10] *The Truth and Meaning of Human Sexuality*, section 78.

[11] *On the Christian Education of Youth [Divini Illius Magistri]* (December 31, 1929), sections 65, 66, and 67.

[12] "It is recommended that parents attentively follow every form of sex education that is given to their children outside the home, *removing their children whenever this education does not correspond to their own principles*" (*The Truth and Meaning of Human Sexuality*, section 117; see also sections 119 and 120).

[13] *The Washington Times*, January 22, 1996, reporting from the annual survey by *Who's Who Among American High School Students*.

[14] Quoted from *Family in America*, published by the Rockford Institute, Rockford, Illinois, February, 1996.

[15] *Journal of Marriage and the Family*, Vol. 56, 1994, pp. 181-192, quoted in *Family in America*, June 1994.

[16] Michael McManus, *Marriage Savers: Helping Your Friends and Family Avoid Divorce* (Grand Rapids, Michigan: Zondervan, 1995), p. 92.

[17] Blankenhorn, *Fatherless America*, p. 46.

[18] *U.S. News & World Report*, July 26, 1993.

[19] See Proverbs 7:1-27 for a good example of a father teaching his son about sexual immorality.

[20] Barbara Dafoe Whitehead, *The Divorce Culture* (New York: Alfred A. Knopf, 1997), p. 156, citing Frank Furstenberg and Christine W. Nord, "Parenting Apart: Patterns of Childbearing After Marital Disruption," *Journal of Marriage and the Family*, 47 (November, 1985), p. 894.

[21] Barbara Dafoe Whitehead, *The Divorce Culture* (New York: Alfred A. Knopf, 1997), p. 156, citing Frank Furstenberg and Andrew J. Cherlin, *Divided Families: What Happens to Children When Parents Part* (Cambridge, Massachusetts: Harvard University Press, 1991), pp. 35-36.

[22] *U.S. News & World Report*, February 10, 1997.

[23] Contact the Family Life Center for a free list of "blocking" software offering protection from sexually explicit Internet sites.

[24] Thirty-three percent of men surveyed at Promise Keepers events in 1994 and in 1996 agreed with the statement, "I enjoy looking at sexually-oriented material." Research by Ken R. Canfield, president, National Center for Fathering, reported in *New Man*, May 1997.

[25] Deuteronomy 10:18; Psalms 10:14, 18; 68:5; 146:9; Jeremiah 49:11. Also see Deuteronomy 24:18, 22 for modeling our fatherhood after the redeeming fatherhood of God.

[26] Contact the Family Life Center for the special January 1997 pro-life edition of the *SJCK Newsletter* suggesting practical things fathers can do to end abortion.

Chapter 9 — Providing for Our Families

[1] For the biblical and historical basis of asking saints in heaven to intercede for us, we suggest Patrick Madrid's *Any Friend of God's is a Friend of Mine: A Biblical and Historical Explanation of the Catholic Doctrine of the Communion of Saints* (San Diego: Basilica Press, 1996).

[2] *USA Today*, May 15, 1996, citing a Louis Harris & Associates survey for the Lutheran Brotherhood.

[3] *Our Sunday Visitor*, May 19, 1996, Letters to Our Sunday Visitor.

[4] See Matthew 4:7, 12:39; Luke 11:29.

[5] Couples beginning to tithe often have questions like, "Do I tithe on my gross, or on my net income?" or "How do I compute my tithe?" In the Old Testament agrarian economy the tithe was easy to compute. Today there are various factors to consider depending upon your profession or the nature of your business. If you want a free fact sheet with examples showing how to compute your tithe, contact the Family Life Center.

[6] Some people think that tithing became obsolete with the coming of Christ and the passing away of the Mosaic Covenant. Tithing is not just linked with the ceremonial laws of the Mosaic Covenant. The first mention of tithing is in Genesis 14, centuries before God's covenant with Moses. In Genesis 14 we find Abraham, the father of all believers, giving a tithe to a priest named Melchizedek. The Epistle to the Hebrews says that Melchizedek prefigured the priesthood of Christ (Hebrews 5-7). What is most interesting is that as Abraham brings his tithe, Melchizedek gives Abraham bread and wine foreshadowing the Eucharist (Genesis 14:18-20). Therefore, if any group of Christians should be good tithers, it should be Catholics who receive the blessings of the Eucharist.

There is one significant difference in tithing between the Old and New Testaments. In the Old Covenant God's people often obeyed God's commands from an external compulsion since the law was only written on tablets of stone. In the New Covenant God's law is written upon the heart enabling all believers to obey God with a strong internal motivation (2 Corinthians 3 and Hebrews 8:6-11). For a treatment on tithing by a Church Council, see *The Canons and Decrees of the Council of Trent*, translated by H. J. Schroeder (Rockford, Illinois, TAN Books, 1978), 25th Session, chapter 12, pp. 245-246. For a good historical survey of tithing in the Old Testament and within the Catholic Church, see *The Catholic Encyclopedia* (New York: The Encyclopedia Press, 1913), Volume 14, pp. 741-742.

[7] We urge families wishing to apply historic Christian principles of financial stewardship to obtain a copy of Philip Lenahan's *Finances for Today's Catholic Family*. Philip Lenahan is the president of Financial Foundations for the Family, an organization offering a wealth of practical financial counseling and resources. Contact Financial Foundations at: P.O. Box 890998, Temecula, CA 92589-0988 for a free tithing brochure and a list of their materials.

8 Credit Counseling Services of New York, Inc., April 16, 1997.

9 Connie Marshner, *Can Motherhood Survive? A Christian Looks At Social Parenting* (Brentwood, Tennessee: Wolgemuth and Hyatt, 1990), p. 219. The personal exemption in 1948 shielded about 75 percent of the average family's income from taxes. Today, the personal exemption shields less than 25 percent of the average family income.

10 Pope John Paul II's address, "The Family and the Economy of the Future," given on March 8, 1996, cited from *L'Osservatore Romano*, March 13, 1996.

11 Article by Richard Hokenson, chief economist for Lufkin and Jenrette Securities, New York, *Barron's*, March 21, 1994. Although the proportion of single-paycheck families is growing, they are still outnumbered by two-paycheck families.

12 Donna Partow, *Homemade Business: A Woman's Step-By-Step Guide to Earning Money at Home* (Colorado Springs, Colorado: Focus on the Family Publishing, 1992); Larry Burkett, *Women Leaving the Workplace* (Chicago: Moody Press, 1995).

13 Lester C. Thurow, professor of economics at MIT, "Changes in capitalism render one-earner families extinct," *USA Today*, January 27, 1997.

14 "Dan Quayle Was Right," *The Atlantic Monthly*, Volume 271 No. 4, April 1993, p. 58.

15 "Dan Quayle Was Right," *The Atlantic Monthly*, Volume 271 No. 4, April 1993, p. 58.

16 "For if the man is the head, the woman is the heart, and as he occupies the chief place in ruling, so she may and ought to claim for herself the chief place in love" (Pope Pius XI's encyclical *Christian Marriage [Casti Connubii]*, 1930).

Chapter 10 — Building Our Marriages and Families on the "Rock"

1 All five of these profound and prophetic documents can be downloaded free from EWTN's Internet address: www.ewtn.com.

2 The new *Catechism of the Catholic Church* says: "Before Christ's second coming the Church must pass through a final trial that will shake the faith of many believers.... The Church will enter the glory of the kingdom only through this final Passover, when she will follow her Lord in his death and Resurrection" (sections 675, 677).

3 John J. Nicola, *Diabolical Possession and Exorcism* (Rockford, Illinois: TAN Books, 1974), p. 151; Ralph Martin, *The Catholic Church at the End of an Age: What is the Spirit Saying?* (San Francisco: Ignatius, 1994), pp. 31-32; Stepfano M. Paci, "Leo XIII's Diabolical Vision," *30 Days* (December, 1990), p. 52; *'Neath St. Michael's Shield* (Boston, Massachusetts: St. Paul Books, 1980), pp. 11-12, 24.

4 *Saint Michael, the Archangel, defend us in battle; be our defense against the wickedness and snares of the devil. May God rebuke him, we humbly pray; and do thou, O Prince of the heavenly host, by the power of*

God, thrust into Hell Satan and the other evil spirits who prowl about the world for the ruin of souls. Leo XIII's vision is reminiscent of Daniel chapter 11, describing the rise of the Antichrist, and chapter 12, describing St. Michael arising to oppose Satan and defend the people of God. No one can say for certain if Pope Leo's mystical experience, his prayer to St. Michael, and the subsequent course of events during the twentieth century indicate the final onslaught of evil in the world. We *can* say that if this century isn't the culmination of evil in the world, then it certainly is a dress rehearsal for that time.

5 *Malcolm Muggeridge on Humanae Vitae* (New York: The National Committee of Catholic Laymen, Inc., 1978).

6 Charles D. Provan, *The Bible and Birth Control* (Monongahela, Pennsylvania: Zimmer Printing, 1989), pp. 62, 68, 81, 91.

7 Janet E. Smith, *Humanae Vitae: A Generation Later* (Washington, D.C.: Catholic University of America Press, 1991), pp. 127, 391. Among spouses teaching NFP with the Couple to Couple League, the divorce rate is 1.4 percent. It is estimated that the divorce rate for all couples using NFP may be up to three times this number, or 4.2 percent, which is still less than a tenth of the national divorce rate.

8 Available at www.ewtn.com.

9 *Catechism of the Catholic Church*, section 2361, quoting *Familiaris Consortio*, section 11.

10 See Genesis 4:1 for an example of the Hebrew verb "to know" (yada / "yaw-dah") being used to describe the marital embrace.

11 Nahum M. Sarna, *The JPS Torah Commentary: Genesis* (New York: The Jewish Publication Society, 1989); G. Alders, *Bible Students Commentary: Genesis*, Volume I (Grand Rapids, Michigan: Zondervan, 1981).

12 For a well-reasoned and comprehensive treatment of how God intended the marital act to renew the marriage covenant, see John F. Kippley's *Sex and the Marriage Covenant: A Basis for Morality* (Cincinnati, Ohio: Couple to Couple League, 1991).

13 Pope John Paul II's *Letter to Families*, section 12.

14 *Catechism of the Catholic Church*, section 2366, quoting *Humanae Vitae*, section 12.

15 *Catechism of the Catholic Church*, sections 2352, 2357, 2399, 2370.

16 For an extensive collection of quotations from Protestant leaders who described the Onan incident as a perverse and immoral sexual act, see Provan, *The Bible and Birth Control*, pp. 62-92. The Old Testament penalty for violating the Levirate Law was not death. See Deuteronomy 25:7-10.

17 Provan, *The Bible and Birth Control*, p. 14, citing Luther's *Commentary on Genesis*.

18 Sigmund Freud, *A General Introduction to Psychoanalysis*, translated by Joan Rivere (Garden City, New York: no publisher, 1935), p. 277, quoted in *Why Humanae Vitae Was Right: A Reader*, edited by Janet Smith (San Francisco: Ignatius Press, 1993), p. 41-42.

[19] *Humanae Vitae*, section 16.

[20] Kippley, *Sex and the Marriage Covenant*, pp. 176, 345.

[21] *Humanae Vitae*, section 16.

[22] *Catechism of the Catholic Church*, section 2368.

[23] *Letter to Families*, section 7.

[24] Psalm 127 and 128.

[25] The spiritual fatherhood of priests in the family of God should be included in a Christian concept of fathering.

[26] *Catechism of the Catholic Church*, sections 2367, 2398.

[27] *Catechism of the Catholic Church*, section 2371.

[28] *Letter to Families*, section 13.

[29] *Letter to Families*, section 13.

[30] Matthew 4:8-10.

[31] David Popenoe, *Life Without Father* (New York: The Free Press, 1996), pp. 3, 19-21; David Blankenhorn, *Fatherless America* (New York: Basic Books, 1995), pp. 18-19.

[32] For anyone with questions about the scriptural and historical basis of the papacy, see Scott Butler, Norman Dahlgren, and David Hess, *Jesus, Peter, and the Keys* (Santa Barbara, California: Queenship Publishing, 1996).

Appendix II — What Scripture Teaches About Divorce and Remarriage

[1] Section 2382.

[2] Section 2384. The catechism supports this statement with a quote from the fourth-century Church Father, St. Basil: "If a husband, separated from his wife, approaches another woman, he is an adulterer because he makes that woman commit adultery; and the woman who lives with him is an adulteress, because she has drawn another's husband to herself."

[3] *Catechism of the Catholic Church*, section 2382.

[4] This interpretation is the faulty basis for the Protestant and Orthodox Churches' view that adultery and other forms of unchastity constitute grounds for divorce. "However, the possibility of divorce on grounds of unchastity, for example, clearly shows that Christ considered that the marriage bond is not absolute: it can be destroyed by sin. The Orthodox Church thus allows divorce as a corrective measure of compassion when a marriage has unfortunately been broken." *The Orthodox Study Bible: New Testament and Psalms*, Fr. Peter E. Gillquist, project director and Alan Wallerstedt, managing editor (Nashville, Tennessee: Thomas Nelson Publishers, 1993), p. 16.

[5] For an explanation of these four exceptions from Leviticus 17-18, see William A. Heth and Gordon J. Wenham, *Jesus and Divorce: The Problem with the Evangelical Consensus* (Carlisle, England: Paternoster Press, 1997), pp. 105-106, 155-165.

6 For a discussion of the seven Noachide laws and their impact on the Council of Jerusalem see: Butler, Dahlgren, and Hess, *Jesus, Peter and the Keys* (Santa Barbara, California: Queenship Publishing, 1996), pp.102-107; and *Catechism of the Catholic Church*, section 58.

7 Volume 1, p. 406.

8 For an excellent summary of the early Church view of marriage, divorce, and remarriage by Protestant Evangelical scholars, see chapter one, *Jesus and Divorce: The Problem With the Evangelical Consensus* by William A. Heth and Gordon J. Wenham (Carlisle, England: Paternoster Press, 1997), pp. 13-44. For the actual texts of the early Church view, see the listing in the doctrinal index on "matrimony" in *The Faith of the Early Fathers*, 3 Volumes, translated by William A. Jurgens (Collegeville, Minnesota: Liturgical Press, 1970).

Recommended Resources

For any of the resources below call toll-free:

1-800-705-6131

Free tape

Call for your *free* audio tape introducing St. Joseph's Covenant Keepers.

Catalog

The Family Life Center offers a *free* catalog of a wide selection of tapes, books and videos on faith, family life, and fatherhood. Many of the books mentioned in the text and in the footnotes of *Christian Fatherhood* are available from our catalog, or by special order through the Family Life Center book service.

Newsletter

St. Joseph's Covenant Keepers Newsletter for Christian fathers is published six times a year. Each issue is packed with relevant and practical tips for contemporary fathers. Call, fax, or e-mail us with your address and we will send you a *free* sample issue.

Small Group Study Guide

A men's small group study guide for *Christian Fatherhood* is available. Call for group discounts on the study guide.

Web Page

Visit the St. Joseph's Covenant Keepers web site at **www.dads.org**.

Conferences

St. Joseph's Covenant Keepers holds men's conferences throughout North America. For a free list of upcoming conferences contact the Family Life Center, or visit our web site. The Family Life Center also sponsors conferences for couples on marriage, parenting, homeschooling, faith, and family life. We also have conferences for parents and teens. To bring a conference to your community, call us for an information pack.

Leadership Training

St. Joseph's Covenant Keepers will host training clinics for men who are going to be teaching the eight commitments to men's small groups. Contact the Family Life Center for scheduled training dates.

Book on Tape

Christian Fatherhood will be available as an audio book after April 1998.

Extra copies of *Christian Fatherhood*

To order extra copies of Christian Fatherhood for your friends, family, small group, or parish, call our toll-free number, 1-800-705-6131 (9 A.M. to 5 P.M. Eastern time), or contact us at:

Family Life Center   Phone: (941) 764-7725
P.O. Box 6060   Fax: (941) 743-5352
Port Charlotte, FL 33949   e-mail: sjck@sunline.net

About the Authors

Stephen Wood

Steve and Karen Wood have been married nineteen years and are the parents of eight children. Steve has led youth, campus, and pro-life ministries. A graduate of Gordon-Conwell Theological Seminary in South Hamilton, Massachusetts, he served as an Evangelical pastor in Florida for a decade before starting the Family Life Center International. Steve is the founder of St. Joseph's Covenant Keepers.

James Burnham

Jim and Lisa Burnham have been married five years and are the parents of three children. Jim is a businessman, the author of *Beginning Apologetics I* and *II,* a lecturer, and the president of San Juan Catholic Seminars.